COSMOPOLITANISM

ETHICS IN A WORLD OF STRANGERS

Issues of Our Time

Ours has been called an information age, but, though information has never been more plentiful, ideas are what shape and reshape our world. "Issues of Our Time" is a series of books in which some of today's leading thinkers explore ideas that matter in the new millennium. The authors—beginning with the philosopher Kwame Anthony Appiah, the lawyer and legal scholar Alan Dershowitz, and the Nobel Prize–winning economist Amartya Sen—honor clarity without shying away from complexity; these books are both genuinely engaged and genuinely engaging. Each recognizes the importance not just of our values but also of the way we resolve the conflicts among those values. Law, justice, identity, morality, and freedom: concepts such as these are at once abstract and utterly close to home. Our understanding of them helps define who we are and who we hope to be; we are made by what we make of them. These are books, accordingly, that invite the reader to reexamine hand-me-down assumptions and to grapple with powerful trends. Whether you are moved to reason together with these authors, or to argue with them, they are sure to leave your views tested, if not changed. The perspectives of the authors in this series are diverse, the voices are distinctive, the issues are vital.

Henry Louis Gates Jr., series editor
W. E. B. Du Bois Professor of the Humanities
Harvard University

Issues of Our Time

Other titles

COSMOPOLITANISM

ETHICS IN A WORLD OF STRANGERS

Kwame Anthony Appiah

W. W. NORTON & COMPANY
NEW YORK • LONDON

For information about permission to reproduce selections from this book, write to
Permissions, W. W. Norton & Company, Inc., 500 Fifth Avenue, New York, NY 10110

Manufacturing by Courier Westford
Book design by Rubina Yeh
Production manager: Julia Druskin

Library of Congress Cataloging-in-Publication Data
Appiah, Anthony.
Cosmopolitanism : ethics in a world of strangers / Kwame Anthony Appiah.— 1st ed.
p. cm. — (Issues of our time)
Includes bibliographical references and index.
ISBN 0-393-06155-8 (hardcover)
1. Ethics. 2. Conduct of life. 3. Cosmopolitanism. I. Title. II. Series.
BJ1031.A63 2006
172—dc22

2005024356

W. W. Norton & Company, Inc., 500 Fifth Avenue, New York, N.Y. 10110
www.wwnorton.com

W. W. Norton & Company Ltd., Castle House, 75/76 Wells Street, London W1T 3QT

1 2 3 4 5 6 7 8 9 0

For my mother, citizen of one world and many

———————

… tibi: namque tu solebas
meas esse aliquid putare nugas.

—Catullus

CONTENTS

INTRODUCTION

MAKING
CONVERSATION

Our ancestors have been human for a very long time. If a normal baby girl born forty thousand years ago were kidnapped by a time traveler and raised in a normal family in New York, she would be ready for college in eighteen years. She would learn English (along with—who knows?—Spanish or Chinese), understand trigonometry, follow baseball and pop music; she would probably want a pierced tongue and a couple of tattoos. And she would be unrecognizably different from the brothers and sisters she left behind. For most of human history, we were born into small societies of a few score people, bands of hunters and gatherers, and would see, on a typical day, only people we had known most of our lives. Everything our long-ago ancestors ate or wore, every tool they used, every shrine at which they worshipped, was made within that group. Their knowledge came from their ancestors or from their own experiences. That is the world that shaped us, the world in which our nature was formed.

Now, if I walk down New York's Fifth Avenue on an ordinary day, I will have within sight more human beings than most of those prehistoric hunter-gatherers saw in a lifetime. Between then and now some of our forebears settled down and learned agriculture; created villages, towns, and, in the end, cities; discovered the power of writing. But it was a slow process. The population of classical Athens when Socrates died, at the end of the fifth century BC, could have lived in a few large skyscrapers. Alexander set off from Macedon to conquer the world three-quarters of a century later with an army of between thirty and forty thousand, which is far fewer people than commute into Des Moines every Monday morning. When, in the first century, the population of Rome reached a million, it was the first city of its size. To keep it fed, the Romans had had to build an empire that brought home grain from Africa. By then, they had already worked out how to live cheek by jowl in societies where most of those who spoke your language and shared your laws and grew the food on your table were people you would never know. It is, I think, little short of miraculous that brains shaped by our long history could have been turned to this new way of life.

Even once we started to build these larger societies, most people knew little about the ways of other tribes, and could affect just a few local lives. Only in the past couple of centuries, as every human community has gradually been drawn into a single web of trade and a global network of information, have we come to a point where each of us can realistically imagine contacting any other of our six billion conspecifics and sending that person something worth having: a radio, an antibiotic, a good idea. Unfortunately, we could also send, through negligence as easily as malice, things that will cause harm: a virus, an airborne pollutant, a bad idea. And the possibilities of good and of ill are multiplied beyond all measure when it comes to policies carried out by governments in our name. Together, we can ruin poor farmers by dumping our subsidized grain into their markets, cripple industries by punitive tariffs, deliver weapons that will kill thousands upon thousands. Together, we can raise standards of living by adopting new policies on trade and aid, prevent or treat diseases with vaccines and pharmaceuticals, take measures against global climate change, encourage resistance to tyranny and a concern for the worth of each human life.

And, of course, the worldwide web of information—radio, television, telephones, the Internet—means not only that we can affect lives everywhere but that we can learn about life anywhere, too. Each person you know about and can affect is someone to whom you have responsibilities: to say this is just to affirm the very idea of morality. The challenge, then, is to take minds and hearts formed over the long millennia of living in local troops and equip them with ideas and institutions that will allow us to live together as the global tribe we have become.

Under what rubric to proceed? Not "globalization"—a term that once referred to a marketing strategy, and then came to designate a macroeconomic thesis, and now can seem to encompass everything, and nothing. Not "multiculturalism," another shape shifter, which so often designates the disease it purports to cure. With some ambivalence, I have settled on "cosmopolitanism." Its meaning is equally disputed, and celebrations of the "cosmopolitan" can suggest an unpleasant posture of superiority toward the putative provincial. You imagine a Comme des Garçons–clad sophisticate with a platinum frequent-flyer card regarding, with kindly condescension, a ruddy-faced farmer in workman's overalls. And you wince.

Maybe, though, the term can be rescued. It has certainly proved a survivor. Cosmopolitanism dates at least to the Cynics of the fourth century BC, who first coined the expression cosmopolitan, "citizen of the cosmos." The formulation was meant to be paradoxical, and reflected the general Cynic skepticism toward custom and tradition. A citizen—a *politēs*—belonged to a particular *polis,* a city to which he or she owed loyalty. The cosmos referred to the world, not in the sense of the earth, but in the sense of the universe. Talk of cosmopolitanism originally signaled, then, a rejection of the conventional view that every civilized person belonged to a community among communities.

The creed was taken up and elaborated by the Stoics, beginning in the third century BC, and that fact proved of critical importance in its subsequent intellectual history. For the Stoicism of the Romans—Cicero, Seneca, Epictetus, and the emperor Marcus Aurelius—proved congenial to many Christian intellectuals, once Christianity became the religion of the Roman Empire. It is profoundly ironic that, though Marcus Aurelius sought to suppress the new Christian sect, his extraordinarily personal *Meditations,* a philosophical diary written in the second century AD as he battled to save the Roman Empire from barbarian invaders, has attracted Christian readers for nearly two millennia. Part of its appeal, I think, has always been the way the Stoic emperor's cosmopolitan conviction of the oneness of humanity echoes Saint Paul's insistence that "there is neither Jew nor Greek, there is neither bond nor free, there is neither male nor female: for ye are all one in Christ Jesus."[1]

Cosmopolitanism's later career wasn't without distinction. It underwrote some of the great moral achievements of the Enlightenment, including the 1789 "Declaration of the Rights of Man" and Immanuel Kant's work proposing a "league of nations." In a 1788 essay in his journal *Teutscher Merkur*, Christoph Martin

Wieland—once called the German Voltaire—wrote, in a character-istic expression of the ideal, "Cosmopolitans . . . regard all the peo-ples of the earth as so many branches of a single family, and the universe as a state, of which they, with innumerable other rational beings, are citizens, promoting together under the general laws of nature the perfection of the whole, while each in his own fashion is busy about his own well-being."[2] And Voltaire himself—whom nobody, alas, ever called the French Wieland—spoke eloquently of the obligation to understand those with whom we share the planet, linking that need explicitly with our global economic interdepend-ence. "Fed by the products of their soil, dressed in their fabrics, amused by games they invented, instructed even by their ancient moral fables, why would we neglect to understand the mind of these nations, among whom our European traders have traveled ever since they could find a way to get to them?"[3]

So there are two strands that intertwine in the notion of cos-mopolitanism. One is the idea that we have obligations to others, obligations that stretch beyond those to whom we are related by the ties of kith and kind, or even the more formal ties of a shared cit-izenship. The other is that we take seriously the value not just of human life but of particular human lives, which means taking an interest in the practices and beliefs that lend them significance. People are different, the cosmopolitan knows, and there is much to learn from our differences. Because there are so many human possibilities worth exploring, we neither expect nor desire that every person or every society should converge on a single mode of life. Whatever our obligations are to others (or theirs to us) they often have the right to go their own way. As we'll see, there will be times when these two ideals—universal concern and respect for legitimate difference—clash. There's a sense in which cosmopoli-tanism is the name not of the solution but of the challenge.

A citizen of the world: how far can we take that idea? Are you really supposed to abjure all local allegiances and partialities in the name of this vast abstraction, humanity? Some proponents of cosmopolitanism were pleased to think so; and they often made easy targets of ridicule. "Friend of men, and enemy of almost every man he had to do with," Thomas Carlyle memorably said of the eighteenth-century physiocrat the Marquis de Mirabeau, who wrote the treatise *L'Ami des hommes* when he wasn't too busy jailing his own son. "A lover of his kind, but a hater of his kindred," Edmund Burke said of Jean-Jacques Rousseau, who handed each of the five children he fathered to an orphanage.

Yet the impartialist version of the cosmopolitan creed has continued to hold a steely fascination. Virginia Woolf once exhorted "freedom from unreal loyalties"—to nation, sex, school, neighborhood, and on and on. Leo Tolstoy, in the same spirit, inveighed against the "stupidity" of patriotism. "To destroy war, destroy patriotism," he wrote in an 1896 essay—a couple of decades before the tsar was swept away by a revolution in the name of the international working class. Some contemporary philosophers have similarly urged that the boundaries of nations are morally irrelevant—accidents of history with no rightful claim on our conscience.

But if there are friends of cosmopolitanism who make me nervous, I am happy to be opposed to cosmopolitanism's noisiest foes. Both Hitler and Stalin—who agreed about little else, save that murder was the first instrument of politics—launched regular invectives against "rootless cosmopolitans"; and while, for both, anti-cosmopolitanism was often just a euphemism for anti-Semitism, they were right to see cosmopolitanism as their enemy. For they both required a kind of loyalty to one portion of humanity—a nation, a class—that ruled out loyalty to all of humanity. And the one thought that cosmopolitans share is that no local loyalty can ever justify forgetting that each human being has responsibilities to every other. Fortunately, we need take sides neither with the nationalist who abandons all foreigners nor with the hard-core cosmopolitan who regards her friends and fellow citizens with icy impartiality. The position worth defending might be called (in both senses) a partial cosmopolitanism.

There's a striking passage, to this point, in George Eliot's *Daniel Deronda*, published in 1876, which was, as it happens, the year when England's first—and, so far, last—Jewish prime minister, Benjamin Disraeli, was elevated to the peerage as Earl of Beaconsfield. Disraeli, though baptized and brought up in the Church of England, always had a proud consciousness of his Jewish ancestry (given the family name, which his father spelled D'Israeli, it would have been hard to ignore). But Deronda, who has been raised in England as a Christian gentleman, discovers his Jewish ancestry only as an adult; and his response is to commit himself to the furtherance of his "hereditary people":

> It was as if he had found an added soul in finding his ancestry—his judgment no longer wandering in the mazes of impartial sympathy, but choosing, with the noble partiality which is man's best strength, the closer fellowship that makes sympathy practical—exchanging that bird's-eye reasonableness which soars to avoid preference and loses all sense of quality, for the generous reasonableness of drawing shoulder to shoulder with men of like inheritance.

Notice that in claiming a Jewish loyalty—an "added soul"—Deronda is not rejecting a human one. As he says to his mother, "I think it would have been right that I should have been brought up with the consciousness that I was a Jew, but it must always have been a good to me to have as wide an instruction and sympathy as possible." This is the same Deronda, after all, who has earlier explained his decision to study abroad in these eminently cosmopolitan terms: "I want to be an Englishman, but I want to understand other points of view. And I want to get rid of a merely English attitude in stud-ies."[4] Loyalties and local allegiances determine more than what we want; they determine who we are. And Eliot's talk of the "closer fellowship that makes sympathy practical" echoes Cicero's claim that "society and human fellowship will be best served if we con-fer the most kindness on those with whom we are most closely associated."[5] A creed that disdains the partialities of kinfolk and community may have a past, but it has no future.

In the final message my father left for me and my sisters, he wrote, "Remember you are citizens of the world." But as a leader of the independence movement in what was then the Gold Coast, he never saw a conflict between local partialities and a universal moral-ity—between being part of the place you were and a part of a broader human community. Raised with this father and an English mother, who was both deeply connected to our family in England and fully rooted in Ghana, where she has now lived for half a cen-tury, I always had a sense of family and tribe that was multiple and overlapping: nothing could have seemed more commonplace.

Surely nothing *is* more commonplace. In geological terms, it has been a blink of an eye since human beings first left Africa, and there are few spots where we have not found habitation. The urge to migrate is no less "natural" than the urge to settle. At the same time, most of those who have learned the languages and customs of other places haven't done so out of mere curiosity. A few were looking for food for thought; most were looking for food. Thoroughgoing ignorance about the ways of others is largely a priv-ilege of the powerful. The well-traveled polyglot is as likely to be among the worst off as among the best off—as likely to be found in a shantytown as at the Sorbonne. So cosmopolitanism shouldn't be seen as some exalted attainment: it begins with the simple idea that in the human community, as in national communities, we need to develop habits of coexistence: conversation in its older meaning, of living together, association.

And conversation in its modern sense, too. The town of Kumasi, where I grew up, is the capital of Ghana's Asante region, and, when I was a child, its main commercial thoroughfare was called Kingsway Street. In the 1950s, if you wandered down it toward the railway yards at the center of town, you'd first pass by Baboo's Bazaar, which sold imported foods and was run by the eponymous Mr. Baboo—a charming and courteous Indian—with the help of his growing family. Mr. Baboo was active in the Rotary and could always be counted on to make a contribution to the various charitable projects that are among the diversions of Kumasi's middle class, but the truth is that I remember Mr. Baboo mostly because he always had a good stock of candies and because he was always smiling. I can't reconstruct the tour down the rest of the street, for not every store had bonbons to anchor my memories. Still, I remember that we got rice from Irani Brothers; and that we often stopped in on various Lebanese and Syrian families, Muslim and Maronite, and even a philosophical Druze, named Mr. Hanni, who sold imported cloth and who was always ready, as I grew older, for a conversation about the troubles of his native Lebanon. There were other "strangers" among us, too: in the military barracks in the middle of town, you could find many northerners among the "other ranks," privates and NCOs, their faces etched in distinctive patterns of ethnic scarification. And then there was the occasional European—the Greek architect, the Hungarian artist, the Irish doctor, the Scots engineer, some English barristers and judges, and a wildly international assortment of professors at the university, many of whom, unlike the colonial officials, remained after independence. I never thought to wonder, as a child, why these people traveled so far to live and work in my hometown; still, I was glad they did. Conversations across boundaries can be fraught, all the more so as the world grows smaller and the stakes grow larger. It's therefore worth remembering that they can also be a pleasure. What academics sometimes dub "cultural otherness" should prompt neither piety nor consternation.

Cosmopolitanism is an adventure and an ideal: but you can't have any respect for human diversity and expect everyone to become cosmopolitan. The obligations of those who wish to exercise their legitimate freedom to associate with their own kind—to keep the rest of the world away as the Amish do in the United States—are only the same as the basic obligations we all have: to do for others what morality requires. Still, a world in which communities are neatly hived off from one another seems no longer a serious option, if it ever was. And the way of segregation and seclusion has always been anomalous in our perpetually voyaging species. Cosmopolitanism isn't hard work; repudiating it is.

In the wake of 9/11, there has been a lot of fretful discussion about the divide between "us" and "them." What's often taken for granted is a picture of a world in which conflicts arise, ultimately, from conflicts between values. This is what we take to be good; that is what they take to be good. That picture of the world has deep philosophical roots; it is thoughtful, well worked out, plausible. And, I think, wrong.

I should be clear: this book is not a book about policy, nor is it a contribution to the debates about the true face of globalization. I'm a philosopher by trade, and philosophers rarely write really useful books. All the same, I hope to persuade you that there are interesting conceptual questions that lie beneath the facts of globalization.

The cluster of questions I want to take up can seem pretty abstract. How real are values? What do we talk about when we talk about difference? Is any form of relativism right? When do morals and manners clash? Can culture be "owned"? What do we owe strangers by virtue of our shared humanity? But the way these questions play out in our lives isn't so very abstract. By the end, I hope to have made it harder to think of the world as divided between the West and the Rest; between locals and moderns; between a blood-less ethic of profit and a bloody ethic of identity; between "us" and "them." The foreignness of foreigners, the strangeness of strangers: these things are real enough. It's just that we've been encouraged, not least by well-meaning intellectuals, to exaggerate their significance by an order of magnitude.

As I'll be arguing, it is an error—to which we dwellers in a scientific age are peculiarly prone—to resist talk of "objective" values. In the absence of a natural science of right and wrong, someone whose model of knowledge is physics or biology will be inclined to conclude that values are not real; or, at any rate, not real like atoms and nebulae. In the face of this temptation, I want to hold on to at least one important aspect of the objectivity of values: that there are some values that are, and should be, universal, just as there are lots of values that are, and must be, local. We can't hope to reach a final consensus on how to rank and order such values. That's why the model I'll be returning to is that of conversation— and, in particular, conversation between people from different ways of life. The world is getting more crowded: in the next half a century the population of our once foraging species will approach nine billion. Depending on the circumstances, conversations across boundaries can be delightful, or just vexing: what they mainly are, though, is inevitable.

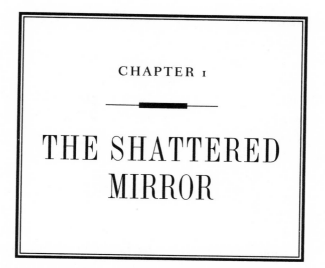

CHAPTER 1

THE SHATTERED MIRROR

A Traveler's Tale

We shall be meeting many cosmopolitans and anti-cosmopolitans in this book, but none, I think, who so starkly combines elements of both as the character who will be the first companion on our journey. Sir Richard Francis Burton was a Victorian adventurer whose life lent credence to that dubious adage about truth being stranger than fiction. Born in 1821, he traveled, as a child, with his family in Europe, and spent time getting to know the Romany people; his English contemporaries liked to say that he had acquired some of the Gypsy's wandering ways. He learned modern Greek in Marseilles and French and Italian, including the Neapolitan dialect, as his family moved between the British expatriate communities of France and Italy; and he arrived at Oxford knowing Béarnais—a language intermediate between French and

Spanish—and (like every other student in those days) classical Greek and Latin as well.

Burton was not just an extraordinary linguist. He was one of the greatest European swordsmen of his day. Before being expelled from Oxford (for ignoring a college ban on going to the races), he challenged a fellow student to a duel because that young man had mocked his walrus mustache. When this fellow didn't grasp that he had been challenged, Burton concluded that he was not among gentlemen but among "grocers." It is just possible, of course, that his adversary was a gentleman who had heard of Burton's prowess with the saber.

At the age of twenty-one, Richard Burton went to work for the East India Company in Sindh, where he added Gujarati, Marathi, Afghan, and Persian to his knowledge of modern and classical European languages, while deepening his mastery of Arabic and Hindi, which he had begun to study in England. Despite being (at least nominally) a Christian, he managed, in 1853, to be admitted to Mecca and Medina as a pilgrim, posing as a Pathan from India's Northwest Frontier Province. He traveled widely in Africa, as well. In 1858, he and John Hanning Speke were the first Europeans to see Lake Tanganyika, and he visited, among other places, Somalia (where he passed as an Arab merchant) as well as Sierra Leone, Cape Coast and Accra (in what is now Ghana), and Lagos. He knew large swaths of Asia and of Latin America; and he translated the *Kama Sutra* from Sanskrit and the *Perfumed Garden* and the *Thousand and One Nights* from Arabic (the latter in sixteen volumes, with a notorious "terminal essay" that included one of the first cross-cultural surveys of homosexuality). Aptly enough, he also translated Luiz Vaz de Camões' *Lusiads*—a celebration of that earlier global explorer Vasco da Gama—from the Portuguese. His translations made him famous (notorious even, when it came to the Oriental erotica); he also wrote grammars of two Indian languages and a vast number of the most extraordinary travel accounts of a century in which there was a good deal of competition in that genre. And, in 1880 he published a long poem that was, he said, a translation of "the *Kasidah* of Haji Abdu El-Yezdi," a native of the desert city of Yazd, in central Persia (one of the few substantial centers of Zoroastrianism remaining in Iran).

A qasida (as we would now write it) is a pre-Islamic classical Arab poetic form, with strict metrical rules, that begins, by tradition, with an evocation of a desert encampment. Although the form was highly respected before the rise of Islam, it saw its heyday in Islam's early days, before the eighth century AD, when it was regarded by some as the highest form of poetic art. But qasida have been written over the centuries through much of the Islamic world, in Turkish and Urdu and Persian as well as in Arabic. Burton's Haji Abdu of Yazd was devoted to "an Eastern Version of Humanitarianism blended with the sceptical or, as we now say, the scientific habit of mind." He was also, as one might guess from reading the poem, a fiction. For though the *Kasidah* is infused with the spirit of Sufism—Islam's mystical tradition—it also alludes to Darwin's evolutionary theory and to other ideas from the Victorian West. Burton, the "translator," offered to explain this by writing, in his notes, that Haji Abdu added

to a natural facility, a knack of language learning, . . . a store of desultory various reading; scraps of Chinese and old Egyptian; of Hebrew and Syriac; of Sanskrit and Prakrit; of Slav, especially Lithuanian; of Latin and Greek, including Romaic; of Berber, the Nubian dialect, and of Zend and Akkadian, besides Persian, his mother-tongue, and Arabic, the classic of the schools. Nor was he ignorant of "the—ologies" and the triumphs of modern scientific discovery.

If the linguistic gifts of this imaginary Sufi read a little too like Burton's own, Burton's conceit was not designed to deceive. At the start of the note, we're told that Abdu "preferred to style himself El-Hichmakâni . . . meaning 'Of No-hall, Nowhere.'" And though Burton's point is, in part, that Haji Abdu is, like himself, a man with no strong sense of national or local identity (dare I say it, a rootless cosmopolitan), it is also, surely, to give us the broadest of hints that El-Yezdi is his own invention.

Certainly the author of the *Kasidah* expressed views that, for a traditional Muslim, are more than mildly heretical. In one stanza he announces,

> There is no Heav'en, there is no Hell;
> these be the dreams of baby minds...

In another he says,

> There is no Good, there is no Bad;
> these be the whims of mortal will...

In short, he can sound—appropriately enough, perhaps, for a native of Zoroastrian Yazd—less like a Persian Sufi and more like Nietzsche's Zarathustra. One thing, though, about the author is not a fiction: since Burton had, in fact, made his pilgrimage to Mecca, the *Kasidah*'s author certainly was a hajji—one who has made the hajj.

Of course, one characteristic of European cosmopolitanism, especially since the Enlightenment, has been a receptiveness to art and literature from other places, and a wider interest in lives elsewhere. This is a reflection of what I called, in the introduction, the second strand of cosmopolitanism: the recognition that human beings are different and that we can learn from each other's differences.

There is Goethe, in Germany, whose career as a poet runs by way of a collection of *Roman Elegies*, written at the end of the 1780s, to the *West-Eastern Divan* of 1819, his last great cycle of poems, inspired by the oeuvre of the fourteenth-century Persian poet Hafiz (author, as Sir Richard Burton would certainly have pointed out, of extremely popular qasida). There is David Hume, in eighteenth-century Edinburgh, scouring traveler's tales, to examine the ways of China, Persia, Turkey, and Egypt. A little earlier still, across the English Channel in Bordeaux, there is Montesquieu, whose monumental *Spirit of the Laws,* published anonymously in Geneva in 1748, is crammed with anecdotes from Indonesia to Lapland, from Brazil to India, from Egypt to Japan; and whose earlier witty satire of his own country, the *Persian Letters*, ventriloquizes a Muslim. Burton's poet, too, seems mostly to speak for Burton: himself an agnostic of a scientific bent, with a vast store of knowledge of the world's religions and an evenhanded assessment of them all.

> All Faith is false, all Faith is true:
> Truth is the shattered mirror strown
> In myriad bits; while each believes
> His little bit the whole to own.

Burton's voracious assimilation of religions, literatures, and customs from around the world marks him as someone who was fascinated by the range of human invention, the variety of our ways of life and thought. And though he never pretended to anything like dispassion, that knowledge brought him to a point where he could see the world from perspectives remote from the outlook in which he had been brought up. A cosmopolitan openness to the world is perfectly consistent with picking and choosing among the options you find in your search. Burton's English contemporaries sometimes thought he displayed more respect for Islam than for the Christianity in which he was raised: though his wife was convinced that he had converted to Catholicism, I think it would be truer to say that he was, as W. H. Wilkins wrote in *The Romance of Isabel Lady Burton*, "a Mohammedan among Mohammedans, a Mormon among Mormons, a Sufi among the Shazlis, and a Catholic among the Catholics."[1]

In this, he follows a long line of itinerant seekers. Menelaus may be most famous as the man the kidnapping of whose wife, Helen, was the casus belli of the Trojan War; but Homer has him boast of having roamed over

> Kypros, Phoinikia, Egypt, and still farther
> among the sun-burnt races.
> I saw the men of Sidon and Arabia
> and Libya, too . . .

where the fecundity of the sheep ensures that "no man, chief or shepherd, ever goes / hungry for want of mutton, cheese, or milk— / all year at milking time there are fresh ewes."[2] Centuries after the *Iliad*, Herodotus writes of how Croesus greeted the wise Solon: "Well, my Athenian friend, I have heard a great deal about your wisdom, and how widely you have travelled in the pursuit of knowledge. I cannot resist my desire to ask you a question: who is the happiest man you have ever seen?" (No "country can produce everything it needs: whatever it has, it is bound to lack something," Solon explains in the course of his reply.)[3] Herodotus himself traveled as far south as present-day Aswan and told us something of Meroë (whose own language has still not been deciphered), a city whose glory days were not to come for another two centuries.

Such exposure to the range of human customs and beliefs hardly left the traveler untethered from his own. Burton illustrates this clearly enough. He was the least Victorian of men, and the most. Certainly he had many of the standard racial prejudices of his society. Africans he ranked below Arabs and most Indians, both of whom were below civilized Europeans. In the third chapter of his *To the Gold Coast for Gold*—an account of a trip to West Africa that began in November 1881—he speaks casually of the "pollution" of Madeiran blood "by extensive miscegenation with the negro."[4] Describing a trip to East Africa in *Blackwood's Edinburgh Magazine* in 1858, he makes similarly unflattering asides: "the negro race is ever loquacious"; "even a Sawahili sometimes speaks the truth"; "Wazira is our rogue, rich in all the peculiarities of African cunning." At one point he turns to a lengthy description of the "Wanika or desert people of the Mombas hills": "All with them is confusion. To the incapacity of childhood they unite the hard-headedness of age." In their religion, he found "the vain terrors of our childhood rudely systematised."[5]

Nor was his capacity for contempt limited to the darker races. He was an odd sort of mélange of cosmopolitan and misanthrope. In his travels across North America through the summer of 1860, recounted in *The City of the Saints, and across the Rocky Mountains to California,* he manages to express hostility to the Irish ("At 9 P.M., reaching 'Thirty-two-mile Creek,' we were pleasantly surprised to find an utter absence of the Irishry"), condescension toward French-Canadians ("a queer lot . . . much addicted to loafing"), distrust of Pawnee Indians ("The Pawnees, African-like, will cut the throat of a sleeping guest"), and gentle mockery of the uniform of the American army ("The States have attempted in the dress of their army, as in their forms of government, a moral impossibility"). Yet he is also capable of composing an elegant defense of a despised people, as in the litany of answers to the "sentimental objections to Mormonism" that runs for many pages of *The City of the Saints.*[6] Still, there is little in Burton's life to suggest that he took seriously what I called in the introduction the first strand of cosmopolitanism: the recognition of our responsibility for every human being. Over and over again in his writings, he passes by opportunities to intervene to reduce human suffering: he records it, sometimes with humor, rarely with outrage. When he needs workers to carry his luggage into the Dark Continent, he buys slaves without a scruple.

Burton is a standing refutation, then, to those who imagine that prejudice derives only from ignorance, that intimacy must breed amity. You can be genuinely engaged with the ways of other societies without approving, let alone adopting, them. And though his *Kasidah* endorsed the kind of spiritualism that was common among the educated upper classes in late Victorian England, its image of the shattered mirror—each shard of which reflects one part of a complex truth from its own particular angle—seems to express exactly the conclusion of Burton's long exposure to the philosophies and the customs of many people and places: you will find parts of the truth (along with much error) everywhere and the whole truth nowhere. The deepest mistake, he supposed, is to think that your little shard of mirror can reflect the whole.

Beyond the Mirror

Life would be easier if we could stop with that thought. We can grant that there's some insight everywhere else and some error *chez nous*. But that doesn't help us when we are trying to decide exactly where the truth lies *this* time. Real disagreements of this kind often arise in the context of religious practices. So let me begin by thinking about one of those practices: the one, in fact, that Richard Burton wrote about so famously.

Most Muslims think they should go to Mecca—making the hajj, if you have the resources, is one of the five pillars of Islam, along with faith in God, charity, fasting, and daily prayer. About one and a half million Muslims make the trip every year. If you're not a Muslim, on the other hand, you don't think that Muhammad was a prophet, and so you are unlikely to think that you yourself should make the hajj. In fact, since unbelievers aren't welcome, what we should probably do is stay away: a tollbooth on the road to Mecca is helpfully signed NO ENTRY FOR NON-MUSLIMS.

Now, this might look, at first glance, like one of those cases where our obligations depend on our positions. You should be faithful to your spouse, we can agree, but *I* don't need to be faithful to your spouse. (In fact, I'd better not be!) Someone might say, in the same spirit, "Muslims should go to Mecca, Catholics to Mass." If you're not a Muslim, though, you don't really think Muslims should go to Mecca, and if you *are* a Muslim, you don't think that anyone, not even a Catholic, has a duty to go to Mass. On the other hand, unless you're some kind of libertine—or a rare survivor of one of those experiments with free love that erupted in the 1960s—you probably think that married people ought to keep their pledges of fidelity to their spouses.

Obviously, Muslims *believe* that they ought to make the hajj and Catholics that they ought to go to Mass. But if you don't have the beliefs that give those acts their meanings, you presumably think that the people who do think so are mistaken. Either Muhammad was *the* Prophet or he wasn't. Either the Koran is *the* definitive Holy Writ or it isn't. And if *he* wasn't and *it* isn't, then Muslims are mistaken. (The same goes, mutatis mutandis, for Mass.) Of course, you probably don't think there's much harm done if people do go to Mecca. They think it's right. We don't. We don't think it's wrong, either, though. Indeed, since we think that integrity matters—that living by your beliefs is important—and since, in this case, there's no harm done in doing what conscience dictates, perhaps it would be a good thing if they made an effort to go.

It's important to insist, however, that to say that Muslims should go to Mecca for this reason isn't to agree with Muslims. It is to give *our* reason for them to do something that they do for a *different* reason. One way of seeing why this matters is to remind ourselves that no self-respecting Muslim would think that you understood, let alone respected, the reason they make the hajj if you said, "Of course you have a reason to go: namely, that you think you should, and people should follow their consciences unless to do so will cause harm." Because that isn't what Muslims think. What they think is that they should go because God commanded it through the Holy Koran. And *that* claim is one that you don't accept at all.

This disagreement is, nevertheless, one that doesn't have to be resolved for us to get along. I can be (indeed, I am!) perfectly friendly with Catholics and Muslims while not always agreeing with them about theology. I have no more reason to resent those who go to Mecca on the hajj than I have to begrudge the choices of those who go to Scotland for golf or to Milan for opera. Not what I'd do, but, hey, suit yourself.

Still, this live-and-let-live attitude is not shared by everyone: some people think that the worship of anyone but the true God is idolatry, itself an offense against divine law, and there are some Christians who think that Allah is not the God of Abraham, Isaac, and Jacob, whom Christians worship. Some Muslims (along with the Unitarians) have worried about whether belief in the Trinity is consistent with Islam's command that we should worship one God. And that possibility draws our attention to a second kind of disagreement.

For there are the cases, of course, where religious practices strike us not as morally indifferent but as actually wrong. Readers of this book are unlikely to think that the proper response to adultery is to take offenders before a religious court and, if they are convicted, to organize a crowd to stone them to death. You and I are no doubt appalled (as are a lot of Muslims, it should be said) by the very thought of a person being stoned to death in this way. Yet many people in the world today think that this is what sharia, Muslim religious law, requires. Or take what we often call female circumcision, which Burton documented among Arabs and East Africans (according to whom, he claimed, sexual desire in women was much greater than in men), and which remains prevalent in many regions. We mostly don't agree with that either. Disagreements like these are perfectly common, even within societies. If you are contemplating an abortion, which *you* think is morally quite permissible, and *I* think that you'll be killing an innocent young human being, I can't just say, "Fine, go ahead," can I?

The temptation is to look for a rule book that could tell you how to arbitrate conflicts like that—but then you'd have to agree on the rule book. And even if you did, for reasons I'll be exploring later, there's no reason to think you'd be able to agree on its application. So there has long been a seductive alternative. Perhaps, even if we agree on all the facts, what's morally appropriate for me to do from my point of view is different from what's morally appropriate for you to do from your point of view. Burton, with his mastery of thirty-nine languages, was something of a freak of nature in his ability to penetrate different cultures—to "go native," as we say, and do so time and time again. But most of us have that ability to some lesser degree: we can often experience the appeal of values that aren't, exactly, our own. So perhaps, when it comes to morality, there is no singular truth. In that case, there's no one shattered mirror; there are lots of mirrors, lots of moral truths, and we can at best agree to differ. Recall the words of Burton's Haji Abdu:

> There is no Good, there is no Bad;
>> these be the whims of mortal will.

Was he right?

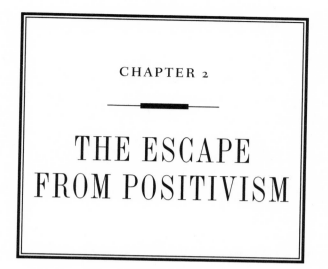

CHAPTER 2

THE ESCAPE
FROM POSITIVISM

Professional Relativism

Cultural anthropologists are great enthusiasts for other cultures. That is, after all, their business. Once, not so long ago, before everybody in the world was within hearing distance of a radio, before Michael Jackson was famous on the steppes of Inner Mongolia and Pele was known along the banks of the Congo River, an anthropologist could set out from Europe or North America for places that had never before seen the "white man." There, at the ground zero of ethnography, the moment of first contact, he or she could come face to face with people who were completely unknown. Their gods, their food, their language, their dance, their music, their carving, their medicines, their family lives, their rituals of peace and war, their jokes and the stories they told their children: all could be wonderfully, fascinatingly strange. Ethnographers spent long days and hard nights in the rain forest or the desert or the tundra, battling fever or frostbite, struggling against loneliness as they tried to make sense of people who were, naturally, equally puzzled by them. And then, after disappearing from "civilization" for a year or two, they would come back with an account of these strangers, bearing (along with a collection of pottery, carvings, or weapons for the museum) a story about how their culture fit together.

For all this to be worthwhile, that story had to be news. So, naturally, the ethnographer didn't usually come back with a report whose one-sentence summary was: they are pretty much like us. And yet, of course, they had to be. They did, after all, mostly have gods, food, language, dance, music, carving, medicines, family lives, rituals, jokes, and children's tales. They smiled, slept, had sex and children, wept, and, in the end, died. And it was possible for this total stranger, the anthropologist, who was, nevertheless, a fellow human being, to make progress with their language and religion, their habits—things that every adult member of the society had had a couple of decades to work on—in a year or two. Without those similarities, how could cultural anthropology be possible?

Now, you might think that anthropologists, whose lives begin with this intellectual curiosity about other peoples, are bound to be cosmopolitans. Not so. While they do share, by necessity, a cosmopolitan curiosity about strangers, many anthropologists mistrust talk about universal morality, and spend a great deal of time urging us not to intervene in the lives of other societies; if they think we have a responsibility, it is to leave well enough alone.

One reason for this skepticism about intervention is simply historical. Much well-intentioned intervention in the past has undermined old ways of life without replacing them with better ones; and, of course, much intervention was not well intentioned. The history of empire—Persian, Macedonian, Roman, Mongol, Hun,

Mughal, Ottoman, Dutch, French, British, American—has many unhappy moments. But there are even broader reasons for the anthropologists' skepticism. What we outsiders see as failings in other societies often make a good deal more sense to the ethnographer who has lived among them. The ethnographer has, after all, set out to make sense of "his" people. And even if there is as much mischief as insight in the old maxim *"Tout comprendre, c'est tout pardonner"*—to understand all is to forgive all—it does reflect a genuine human tendency. We often *do* forgive, once we understand. Anthropologists are likely, as a result, to find many outside interventions ignorant and uninformed. We think female circumcision, or female genital cutting, as many anthropologists prefer to call it, a disgusting mutilation that deprives women of the full pleasures of sexual experience. They know young women who look forward to the rite, think that it allows them to display courage, declare it makes their sexual organs more beautiful, and insist that they enjoy sex enormously. They will point out that our society encourages all kinds of physical alterations of human bodies—from tattoos and ear (and now tongue, nose, and umbilicus) piercing to male circumcision to rhinoplasty to breast augmentation—and that each of these practices, like all bodily alterations, has some medical risks. They will show us that the medical risks allegedly associated with female genital cutting—scarring, infections leading to infertility, fatal septicemia—have been wildly exaggerated; that they are, perhaps, just rationalizations for what is simply revulsion against an unfamiliar practice. In contrast to us, they feel, they have escaped the prejudices of their backgrounds, in part through the intellectual discipline of fieldwork, living intimately with strangers. And many of them are inclined to think that words like "right" and "wrong" make sense only relative to particular customs, conventions, cultures.

Certainly the basic suspicion that moral claims just reflect local preferences is age-old. In book three of Herodotus's *Histories*, we read that when Darius

> was king of Persia, he summoned the Greeks who happened to be present at his court, and asked them what they would take to eat the dead bodies of their fathers. They replied that they would not do it for any money in the world. Later, in the presence of the Greeks, and through an interpreter, so that they could understand what was said, he asked some Indians, of the tribe called Callatiae, who do in fact eat their parents' dead bodies, what they would take to burn them. They uttered a cry of horror and forbade him to mention such a dreadful thing. One can see by this what custom can do, and Pindar, in my opinion, was right when he called it "king of all."[1]

One of Tolstoy's stories is about a Chechen warlord called Hadji Murat, who tells a Russian officer one of his people's traditional sayings: "'A dog asked a donkey to eat with him and gave him meat, the donkey asked the dog and gave him hay: they both went hungry.' He smiled. 'Every people finds its own ways good.'"[2]

And doubtless there is something salutary about the ethnographic inclination to pause over our own abominations and taboos. In the 1906 classic *Folkways*, the anthropologist William G. Sumner tells of a chief of the Miranhas, in the Amazon, who is baffled that Europeans regard cannibalism as an abomination: "It is all a matter of habit. When I have killed an enemy, it is better to eat him than to let him go to waste. Big game is rare because it does not lay eggs like turtles. The bad thing is not being eaten, but death."[3] Sumner, who coined the term "ethnocentrism," was not himself recommending cannibalism. But he clearly had sympathy for the chief's account: *chacun à son goût.*

Or, in the words of Burton's fictive Sufi,

> What works me weal that call I "good,"
> What harms and hurts I hold as "ill":
> They change with place, they shift with race;
> And, in the veriest span of Time,
> Each Vice has won a Virtue's crown;
> All good was banned as Sin or Crime.

Yet the modern doctrines of relativism—the approach that cultural anthropologists often subscribe to—go beyond the old skeptical traditions. A lingering suspicion that a lot of what we take to be right and wrong is simply a matter of local custom has hardened, in the modern age, into a scientific certainty that talk of objective moral "truths" is just a conceptual error.

The Exile of Value

What grounds modern relativism is a scientific worldview that makes a sharp distinction between *facts* and *values*. John Maynard Keynes used to say that those who claimed that they were just talking common sense were often simply in the grip of an old theory. This distinction between facts and values is now commonsense, but behind it is a philosophical theory that goes back at least to the early Enlightenment. Its origins have sometimes been traced to the eighteenth-century Scottish philosopher David Hume, whose cosmopolitan engagement with the variety of human societies I mentioned in the last chapter. As it happens, I doubt that Hume would have endorsed this theory (or, indeed, that he invented it), but something very like this view was certainly current in the twentieth-century heyday of a philosophical movement called logical positivism, so I'm going to call it Positivism.

The picture took a while to develop, but here it is, in a simplified, final version.

It is never easy to sketch a philosophical position, least of all to the satisfaction of those who claim it as their own. So I should make it plain that I am not trying to characterize the view of this or that philosopher, however influential, but rather a picture of the world, elaborated by many philosophers over the last few centuries in the West, that has now so penetrated the educated common sense of our civilization that it can be hard to persuade people that it *is* a picture and not just a bunch of self-evident truths. That would not matter, of course, if the picture never got in the way of our understanding the world. But, as we shall see, the Positivist picture *can* get in the way; in particular, it often gets in the way of the cosmopolitan project, when it leads people to overestimate some obstacles to cross-cultural understanding while underestimating others.

What people do, Positivism holds, is driven by two fundamentally different kinds of psychological states. Beliefs—the first kind—are supposed to reflect how the world is. Desires, by contrast, reflect how we'd like it to be. As the philosopher Elizabeth Anscombe once put it, beliefs and desires have different "directions of fit": beliefs are meant to fit the world; the world is meant to fit desires. So beliefs can be true or false, reasonable or unreasonable. Desires, on the other hand, are satisfied or unsatisfied.

Beliefs are supposed to be formed on the basis of evidence, and there are principles of reasoning that determine what it is rational to believe on the basis of what evidence. Desires are just facts about us. In an earlier philosophical language, indeed, these desires would have been called "passions," from a Latin root meaning something you suffer, or undergo (a meaning still left to us in talk of the Passion of Christ). Because passions are just things that happen to us, no evidence determines which ones are right. All desires, in fact, are just like matters of taste; and, as the saying goes, there's no accounting for those. When we act, we use our beliefs about the world to figure out how to get what we desire. Reason, as Hume famously said, is "the slave of the passions." If our passion is for apples, we go to where our beliefs suggest the apples are. And, once we go looking for the apples we're after, we'll find out whether our beliefs were right.

Because beliefs are about the world, and there's only one world, they can be either right or wrong, and we can criticize other people's beliefs for being unreasonable or simply false. But desires can't be right or wrong, in this sense. Desires are simply not responses to the world; they're aimed at changing it, not at reflecting how it is.

There's a complication to the story, because much of what we ordinarily desire has beliefs, so to speak, built into it. Like you, I want money; but only because of what it can get me. If I didn't believe that money could get me other stuff that I wanted, I wouldn't want it any more. So my desire for money (I'd rather not call it a passion, if you don't mind) is *conditional*; it would disappear, if I discovered— as I might in some apocalyptic scenario—not only that money can't buy me love (this I have known since my first Beatles concert), but that it couldn't buy me anything at all. Desires that are conditional in this way can be rationally criticized by criticizing the underlying beliefs. I want an apple. You tell me I'm allergic and it will make me sick. I say: I don't mind being sick, if I can just have that delicious taste. You tell me that this apple won't have that delicious taste. I say: Find me something that will. You say: The only things that have that taste will kill you. I say: So be it. It will be worth it. I die happy. It looks as if nothing in the world can stop me from wanting that taste. On the Positivist picture, this is the only way desires can be criticized: by criticizing beliefs they presuppose. Once you remove the conditional element from the specification of a desire, you get to what we might call your *basic desires*. And since these depend on *no* assumptions about how the world is, you can't criticize them for getting the world wrong. So the fundamental point remains.

Hume himself drew the distinction, in a famous passage, between judgments about how things are and judgments about how things ought to be. Normative judgments naturally come with views about what one ought to think, do, or feel. And the Positivist picture is often thought to be Humean in part because Hume insisted that the distinction between "is" and "ought" was, as he said, "of the last consequence." Like desires, *oughts* are intrinsically action guiding, in a way that *is* isn't. And so, in the familiar slogan, "you can't get an ought from an is." Since we are often tempted to move from what is to what ought to be, this move, like many moves philosophers think illicit, has a disparaging name: we call it the *naturalistic fallacy*.

Such a distinction between the way beliefs and desires work in action is the key to this picture of how human beings work. Desires—or, more precisely, basic desires—set the ends we aim for; beliefs specify the means for getting to them. Since these desires can't be wrong or right, you can criticize only the means people adopt, not their ends. Finally, the Positivist identifies the truths that beliefs aim at with the facts. If you believe something and your belief is true, it gets one of the facts in the world right.

If that's what facts are on the Positivist view, what are values? You could say that, strictly speaking, the Positivist thinks there aren't any values. Not, at least in the world. "The world," the young Ludwig Wittgenstein said, "is the totality of facts." After all, have you ever seen a value out there in the world? As the philosopher John L. Mackie used to argue, values, if there were any, would be very strange entities. ("Queer" was the word he used: and his argument that there aren't really any values in the world he called "the argument from queerness.") The world can force us to believe in *things*, because if we don't they'll bump into us anyhow, get in our way. But reality can't force us to desire anything. Where, after all, would one look in the world for the wrongness of a basic desire? What science would demonstrate it? A science might be able to explain why you desire something. It couldn't explain that you should—or shouldn't—desire it.

Talk of values, then, is really a way of talking about certain of our desires. Which ones? Well, when we appeal to what we take to be universal values in our discussions with one another—the value of art or of democracy or of philosophy—we're talking about things we want everyone to want. If exposure to art is valuable, then, roughly, we'd like everyone to want to experience it. If we say democracy is valuable, then, roughly again, we want everyone to want to live in a democracy. We might say, as a *façon de parler*, that someone who wants everyone to want X "believes that X is valuable," but that is still just, in reality, a way of talking about a complex desire. Again, some values will subsist upon certain facts. I could value universal vaccination for smallpox, because I wanted to make everyone safer—but give up this "value" once I learned that smallpox had been eradicated. If a value reflects unconditional desires, however, since these basic desires can't be criticized, values can't either. I value kindness. I want to be kind. I want me to want to be kind. I want all of you to want to be kind. As a matter of fact, I want *you* to want everyone to want to be kind. But I don't want this because I believe that all these kindnesses will lead to something else. I value kindness intrinsically, unconditionally. Even if you showed me that some acts of kindness would have effects I didn't want, that wouldn't persuade me to give up kindness as a value. It would only show me that kindness can sometimes conflict with other things I care about.

It may be that there are basic desires like this that everyone has. So it may turn out that there are things that everyone values. Those values will be *empirically* universal. Still, on the Positivist view, there's no rational basis on which to establish that they're correct.

If you accept that all this is a fair, if sketchy, version of a philosophical account that has been extremely influential for at least the last two and a half centuries in the West, you'll see that many of the consequences of thinking in this way are recognizable parts of our common sense. There are facts and there are values. *Check.* Unlike values, facts—the things that make beliefs true and false—are the natural inhabitants of the world, the things that scientists can study or that we can explore with our own senses. *Check.* So, if people in other places have different basic desires from people around here—and so have different values—that's not something that we can rationally criticize. No appeal to reasons can correct them. *Check.* And if no appeal to reasons can correct them, then trying to change their minds must involve appeal to something other than reason: which is to say, to something unreasonable. There seems no alternative to relativism about fundamental values. *Checkmate.*

I don't know how sensible this picture of human reasoning seems to you, but it grabbed the imaginations of many students of other cultures. That's why the great anthropologist Melville Herskovits once wrote, "There is no way to play this game of making judgments across cultures except with loaded dice."[4] Yet it has implications that are inconsistent with what most of us believe. A Tormentor who wanted everyone to want to cause innocent people pain, we might say, takes the infliction of pointless suffering to be a value. We'd also want to say that he was wrong. Do we have to content ourselves with the Positivist view that our judgment *just* reflects our desires, as the Tormentor's reflects his?

Positivist Problems

There are various moves critics of Positivism have proposed in response to such challenges. One is, so to speak, to go on the offensive. There are lots of facts that one can't point to and lots of beliefs that we don't have evidence for (if that means evidence from experience, from seeing, hearing, tasting, smelling, touching). If every true belief corresponds to a fact, then isn't it a fact that one and one make two? Where exactly is *that* fact? And what's the *evidence* that bachelors can't be married? However many unmarried bachelors you find, that won't show you that bachelors *can't* be married. So far as I know, no one has ever found a pine tree with exactly fifty-seven cones painted purple and gold. Still, nobody thinks there couldn't be one. For that matter, who could deny that, as Socrates insisted, all men are mortal? So where is *that* fact?

The Positivist picture, in short, seems to generalize too quickly from one kind of belief: beliefs about the properties of particular concrete things that you can see, hear, touch, smell, or feel. What are we to say about beliefs about universals (all human beings), about possibilities and impossibilities (married bachelors), and about abstract objects (the number two)? The Positivist seems to be suggesting that if we can't answer the question "Where is that fact?" or meet the command "Show me the evidence," then there can't be any true beliefs about that subject matter. Every true belief corresponds to a fact "out there" in the world, the Positivist claims. But then we'd have to abandon belief not only in values but also in possibilities, numbers, universal truths, and, one suspects, a whole lot more. A theory that sounded plausible to begin with now looks as if it comes with a pretty high price tag. It's not that the Positivists don't have theories about numbers and universals and possibilities. It's that once you grasp that you have to tell a lot of different stories about different kinds of truths, the idea that observable facts are what truths correspond to looks a good deal less obvious.

There is another fundamental puzzle for the Positivist. The Positivist thinks that you can criticize beliefs and actions as unreasonable. Okay. Is it a *fact* that they're unreasonable? If it is, then can't we ask about *that* fact what the Positivist asked when we claimed that causing innocent people pain was wrong? Where is it? Where, for example, is the *fact* that it's unreasonable to believe that something that looks green is actually red? And what evidence supports the claim that it's unreasonable to believe that something's green when it looks red? Someone who thinks this is reasonable is hardly going to be persuaded by our showing him red-looking things and insisting they are red. These questions look just as hard for the Positivist as the ones he posed to us.

If, on the other hand, it isn't a *fact* that certain beliefs are unreasonable, then, presumably, it's a *value*. (For the Positivist, those are the only options.) So to say, "It's unreasonable to believe that what looks green is red," just means that you want everybody to want not to think that what looks green is red. And if it's a basic value, then it can't be critically evaluated. The Positivist has no rational objection to make to people who make this preposterous assertion. But surely people who think red-looking things are green aren't just pursuing an "alternative lifestyle" with its own values. They're irrational, and they ought not to think that way.

There's a disconnect, too, between the Positivist creed and the relativist counsel that we ought not to intercede in other societies on behalf of our own values. For on the Positivist account, to value something is, roughly, to want everyone to want it. And if that's the case, then values are, in a certain way, naturally imperialist. So the whole strategy of arguing for toleration of other cultures on the basis of Positivism seems self-contradictory. How can you argue rationally that other people's basic value choices should be tolerated on the basis of a view that says that there are no rational arguments for such basic choices? Positivism doesn't motivate intervention; but it doesn't motivate nonintervention, either. (One may be reminded of an old story from the days of colonial India. A British officer who was trying to stop a suttee was told by an Indian man, "It's our custom to burn a widow on her husband's funeral pyre." To which the officer replied, "And it's our custom to execute murderers.")

Some relativists confuse two different senses in which judgments can be *subjective*. The view that moral judgments express desires means that they are, in one sense, subjective. Which judgments you will agree to depends on what desires you have, which is a feature of you. But, in this sense, factual judgments are subjective also. Which ones you will accept depends on what beliefs you have, which is similarly a feature of you. From the fact that beliefs are subjective in this way, therefore, it does not follow that they are subjective in the sense that you are *entitled* to make any judgments you like. Indeed, to go from the first claim to the second is to make one of those moves from "is" to "ought" that furrowed Hume's brow. It's to commit the naturalistic fallacy. So even on the Positivist view there is no route from the subjectivity of value judgments to a defense of toleration. Toleration is just another value.

Values Reclaimed

What's an alternative to the Positivist picture of values? Values guide our acts, our thoughts, and our feelings. These are our *responses* to values. Because you recognize the value of great art, you go to museums and to concert halls and read books. Because you see the value of courtesy, you try to understand the conventions of each society that you live in so that you can avoid giving offense. You act as you do because you respond to the values that guide you. And values shape thought and feeling as well. Truth and reason, values you recognize, shape (but, alas, do not determine) your beliefs. Because you respond, with the instinct of a cosmopolitan, to the value of elegance of verbal expression, you take pleasure in Akan proverbs, Oscar Wilde's plays, Basho's haiku verses, Nietzsche's philosophy. Your respect for wit doesn't just lead you to these works; it shapes how you respond to them. Just so, valuing kindness leads you to admire some gentle souls, and leaves you irritated by other thoughtless ones. It's true that when you think of, say, kindness, as a universal value, you want everybody to want to be kind. And, since you want them to agree with you, you also want *them* to want everybody to want everybody to be kind. But perhaps the Positivist has the story exactly the wrong way round. Perhaps you want people to want each other to be kind *because you recognize the value of kindness.* You want people to agree with you because people who agree with you will be kind and encourage kindness in others. The same thing is true about everything you hold to be a universal value, a basic human good: your valuing it is a judgment that we all have a good reason to do or to think or to feel certain things in certain contexts, and so, also, have reason to encourage these acts and thoughts and feelings in others.

How, in fact, do people learn that it is good to be kind? Is it by being treated kindly and noticing that they like it? Or by being cruelly treated and disliking it? That doesn't seem quite right: kindness isn't like chocolate, where you find whether you have a taste for it by giving it a try. Rather, the idea that it's a good seems to be part of the very concept. Learning what kindness is means learning, among other things, that it's good. We'd suspect that someone who denied that kindness was good—or that cruelty was bad—didn't really understand what it was. The concept itself is value-laden, and therefore action guiding.

The Positivist will no doubt ask us what we will do about the ones who think cruelty good. And I think the right answer is that we should do with them what we should do with people who think that red things are green. Faced with the Tormentor who genuinely thinks it good to be cruel, the Positivist has just the options we have. Change the Tormentor's mind. Keep out of his way. Keep him out of ours.

Disagreements of this fundamental sort are actually quite unusual. You have probably never met someone who sincerely admits to thinking that it's just fine to be cruel to ordinary innocent human beings. There are people who think that it is okay to be cruel to animals. There are people who favor cruelty to wicked people. There are people who don't recognize what they are doing is cruel. And there are people who think that cruelty can be justified by other considerations. Many people think torture can be a necessary evil to uncover terrorist plots. Still, it is, exactly, as a necessary *evil,* a bad thing done in the service of a greater good. Defending particular acts of cruelty in this way means that you recognize the value of avoiding cruelty if you can.

The deepest problem with Positivism, however, is not in its conclusions. It is in its starting point. I began, as I think one must if one is to make the Positivist story believable, with a single person, acting on her own beliefs and desires. Starting from there, one has to give an account of values that begins with what it is for me—this single person—to regard something as valuable. But to understand how values work, you must see them not as guiding us as individuals on our own but as guiding people who are trying to share their lives.

The philosopher Hilary Putnam famously argued that, as he once put it, "Meanings ain't in the head." You can talk about elm trees, even if you personally couldn't tell an elm from a beech; you can talk about electrons, even if you couldn't give a very good account of what they are. And the reason you can use these words—and *mean* something by them—is that other people in your language community do have the relevant expertise. There are physicists who are experts on electronics, naturalists who know all about elms. Our use of factual terms like these depends upon these social circumstances. What I mean doesn't depend only on what's in my brain.

We go astray, similarly, when we think of a moral vocabulary as the possession of a solitary individual. If meanings ain't in the head, neither are morals. The concept of kindness, or cruelty, enshrines a kind of social consensus. An individual who decides that kindness is bad and cruelty good is acting like Lewis Carroll's Humpty-Dumpty, for whom a word "means just what I choose it to mean—neither more, nor less." The language of values is, after all, language. And the key insight of modern philosophical reflection on language is that language is, first and foremost, a public thing, something we share. Like all vocabulary, evaluative language is primarily a tool we use to talk to one another, not an instrument for talking to ourselves. You know what you call someone who uses language mostly to talk to himself? Crazy.

Our language of values is one of the central ways we coordinate our lives with one another. We appeal to values when we are trying to get things done *together*. Suppose we are discussing a movie. You say that it expresses a cynical view of human nature. This is not just an invitation to me to accept a fact about the film's picture of the characters and their motivations; it is also an attempt to shape how I feel. Seeing it that way, I am more likely, for example, to resist my first emotional responses, my sympathy, say, with certain characters. If I hold on to those feelings, I might want to resist your characterization. Not cynical, I might say; pessimistic, for sure, but also deeply humane. *Cynical, humane, pessimistic:* these are part of the vocabulary of value. And, as I say, they are meant to shape our responses.

Why, you might ask, should we care how other people think and feel about stories? Why do we talk about them in this language of value? One answer is just that it is part of being human. People tell stories and discuss them in every culture, and we know they have done so back as far as the record goes. The *Iliad* and the *Odyssey*, the *Epic of Gilgamesh*, the *Tale of Genji*, the Ananse stories I grew up with in Asante, weren't just read or recited: they were discussed, evaluated, referred to in everyday life. We wouldn't recognize a community as human if it had no stories, if its people had no narrative imagination. So one answer to the question why we do it is: it's just one of the things that humans do.

But a deeper answer is that evaluating stories together is one of the central human ways of learning to align our responses to the world. And that alignment of responses is, in turn, one of the ways we maintain the social fabric, the texture of our relationships. The 2004 Afghan film *Osama,* which tells the story of the life of a girl under the Taliban, shows us women and girls driven out of public life to hide in the shadows, as murderous and moralizing mullahs seek to impose a vision of gender they claim to derive from Islam. It shows us the waste of human talent: Osama's mother is a doctor who cannot practice. It shows us, too, that there are women who find small ways of resisting, and men who are forced into acts of courage as well as moments of dishonesty to help them. And it reminds us, at the end, when Osama is handed over to be the latest of four unwilling wives of an elderly mullah, that what makes oppression possible is that there are people who profit as well as people who suffer. Robbing Peter to pay Paul, as George Bernard Shaw observed shrewdly, is a policy that will, at least, guarantee you the vigorous support of Paul.

Our response to this film, when we discuss it with one another, reinforces our common understanding, and the values we share. *Murderous, waste, courage, dishonesty, oppression:* these are value terms, meant to shape our responses to the movie. And if the story it tells is truly representative, our discussion of it will help us decide not only what we feel about the characters but how we should act in the world. Talk about *Osama* can help us think about whether it was right for so many of the nations of the world to unite to remove the Taliban regime. It helps us, too, to think about other kinds of oppression, other places for courage, other wasted opportunities. It keeps our vocabulary of evaluation honed, ready to do its work in our lives. And that work, as I say, is first to help us act together.

You could insist on a technical use of the word "reason" to mean something like "calculation," which is what it seems to mean when modern Positivists use it. And then it would be fine to say that when people talk in these ways they are not, strictly speaking, reasoning together. But in the English we speak every day, it is natural to call what we do when we seek, through a conversation rich in the language of value, to shape each other's thoughts and sentiments and deeds, "offering reasons."

Folktales, drama, opera, novels, short stories; biographies, histories, ethnographies; fiction or nonfiction; painting, music, sculpture, and dance: every human civilization has ways to reveal to us values we had not previously recognized or undermine our commitment to values that we had settled into. Armed with these terms, fortified with a shared language of value, we can often guide one another, in the cosmopolitan spirit, to shared responses; and when we cannot agree, the understanding that our responses are shaped by some of the same vocabulary can make it easier to agree to disagree. All this is part of the truth about human life. And it is a part of the truth that Positivism makes it very hard to see.

For if relativism about ethics and morality were true, then, at the end of many discussions, we would each have to end up saying, "From where I stand, I am right. From where you stand, you are right." And there would be nothing further to say. From our different perspectives, we would be living effectively in different worlds. And without a shared world, what is there to discuss? People often recommend relativism because they think it will lead to tolerance. But if we cannot learn from one another what it is right to think and feel and do, then conversation between us will be pointless. Relativism of that sort isn't a way to encourage conversation; it's just a reason to fall silent.

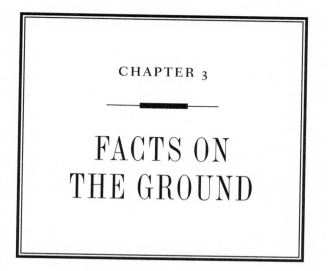

CHAPTER 3

FACTS ON THE GROUND

Living with Spirits

L ate one evening, at home in Ghana many years ago, I was watching television with my father. As the broadcast day came to a close, the Ghana Broadcasting Corporation played the national anthem. My father loved hymns, and so he sang along. "God bless our homeland, Ghana . . ." As the singing ended and the screen faded to the test card, he remarked that he was glad that the government had modified the words of the independence national anthem, which I had learned in primary school. That one began, "Lift high the flag of Ghana." I was a newly minted philosophy graduate at the time, who had recently read John Rawls's modern liberal classic, *A Theory of Justice,* and my response was to say that the old anthem had the advantage that you could sing along with it happily without believing in God. My father laughed. "Nobody in Ghana is silly enough not to believe in God," he said.

That's not how I would have put it; but it's true that Ghana's atheists could hold their meetings in a phone booth. Almost everybody in Ghana believes not just in a powerful divine creator but in a whole range of other spirits. One reflection of this belief is that at funerals, naming ceremonies, marriages, confirmations, birthday parties—indeed, at almost any social gathering—people of all religions will pour libations to their ancestors. When they open a bottle of whisky or gin or schnapps, they will pour some on the ground and ask various dead ancestors, by name, to accept the offering and to keep watch over the interests of the *abusua*, the matriclan. This is not just a symbolic gesture. While they don't think the ancestors literally need liquor, they do think they, and other largely invisible spirits, can hear and respond by helping their living relatives in everyday life. My father—a member of one of the London Inns of Court; an elder in the Methodist church of Ghana; a man whose favorite bedside reading, apart from the Bible, was Cicero—certainly believed this. And he wasn't embarrassed by the fact. His autobiography is full of episodes in which he sought and received the assistance of spirits. When he opened a bottle of whisky at home, after pouring off a little onto the floor of the sitting room, he would speak some words to Akroma-Ampim, an eighteenth-century Asante general who laid the foundations of the family fortune, and Yao Antony, my great-great-uncle (both of whose names, as it happens, I bear), as well as to my great-great-aunt, Yao Antony's sister.

If this were all symbolic, we could suppose that these acts expressed family values or something of the sort. The trouble is the fundamental belief wasn't remotely symbolic. If you don't think your late great-uncle could hear you and help you in your doings, you disagree with my father about the facts.

Here's another thing about which you are likely to disagree with my Ghanaian kin. Most of them believe in witchcraft. They think that there are certain evil people—women and men—who have the power to harm others they dislike without using ordinary everyday means. When my father died, one of my sisters was convinced that an aunt of ours might be practicing witchcraft against us. She wouldn't eat any of the food that our aunt sent us during the period of mourning, and she wouldn't let the rest of the family eat it either. But she thought it was fine for other people in the household to eat it. It wasn't poisoned. Witchcraft medicines know the difference between the people they're aimed at and the ones they're not; the food would harm only us. Since my aunt was supposed to be a powerful witch, this wasn't the only danger we faced. So it was fortunate that there are also practitioners of good witchcraft—many of them Muslim *malaams*, actually—who could counteract bad witchcraft. My sister made sure we bought a white ram to be sacrificed to protect us.

Asante beliefs about spirits and beliefs about witchcraft are extensive, complex, and interconnected. And, as you'd expect, not everybody believes exactly the same things about them. Some evangelical Christians identify the traditional spirits—whose shrines and priests you will find scattered through the country—with devils or with what the New Testament, in the King James translation, calls "principalities and powers." Not so my father, who took his appeals to spirits to be consistent with his Methodism. You could say that most people in Asante believe in a sort of theory, in which the world contains many spirits and invisible forces that work, like witchcraft, to affect human life. And, since some of the theory is about invisible personal beings—to whom you can pray for help—you might also say that it was part of Asante religion.

Of course, the place where I grew up is, in this way, like most places in the world. Even where the great world religions—

Christianity, Islam, Hinduism, Buddhism—have come in, they overlie a set of traditions that include all kinds of invisible spirits who can be invoked both to do good and to do harm.

Now, the Positivist is likely to contrast these beliefs with modern scientific views. "These traditional religions are not just false, they are irrational: anyone who exposed them to the rigorous examination that scientists practice would be forced to give them up." This is, in fact, very far from evident. In the last chapter, I argued that values aren't as flighty as the Positivist supposes. Here I want to suggest that facts aren't quite so solid. Not because I'm a skeptic about truth. (I once wrote a book called *For Truth in Semantics*.) But because finding the truth isn't just a matter of having open eyes and a level head.

Arguing with Akosua

Take the simple-seeming question of whether you can be harmed by witchcraft. How would you go about persuading one of my Asante kinfolk that it could not be? People do get sick for unaccountable reasons all the time, do they not? Many of them have reason to think that there are people who dislike them. So that once you have the idea of witchcraft, there will be plenty of occasions when the general theory will seem to be confirmed. To rule out the theory of witchcraft, you would first have to understand it better, and then you would have to persuade my relatives both that the theory gets it wrong over and over again and that you have a better story. That could take a very long time. In a real cross-cultural encounter of this sort, you would be invited to explain all sorts of facts you were unaware of, whose explanations you did not know. Akosua, your Asante interlocutor, has an aunt who fell ill last year, and everyone knows that it was caused by witchcraft by her daughter-in-law. The family went to a *malaam* and slaughtered a sheep. She got better. Akosua wants to know why her aunt got better, if the sheep had nothing to do with it; why she got ill, if there's no witchcraft. And, of course, while you think that these questions have answers, you don't know for sure what they are.

On the other hand, you have to persuade Akosua of the existence of tiny, invisible atoms, strung together to make viruses, particles so small that you cannot see them with the most powerful magnifying lens, yet so potent that they can kill a healthy adult. Consider how long it took to persuade European scientists that this was so, how complex the chain of inferences that led first to the germ theory of disease and then to the identification of viruses. Why should anyone believe this story, just because you said so? And could you— and I mean you, not some biology professor—provide her with convincing evidence? Akosua might well be willing to do one of the experiments you propose. You might, for example, try to show that there's no correlation between whether someone who is thought to be a witch hates you and whether you fall sick. But what if there *were* such a correlation? If Akosua's view made the right prediction—that people who are hated by witches get sicker more often than people who aren't—you wouldn't come to believe in witchcraft. You'd have an alternative explanation. (People who think they are hated by powerful witches might well be more likely to fall ill, mightn't they? Something to do with stress, perhaps?) So it shouldn't surprise you that when your predictions are borne out, she has her explanations, too.

There's an oft-told anecdote about a medical missionary in a remote place, who watches, in horror, as people give untreated well water to their babies. The children regularly get diarrhea, and many of them die. The missionary explains that, even though the water looks clear, there are tiny, invisible creatures in it that make the children sick. Fortunately, she says, if they boil the water, it will kill these bacteria. A month later she's back, and they're still giving the babies the dirty water. After all, if a stranger came into your community and told you that your children got influenza because of witchcraft, would you respond by going out and slaughtering a sheep? Then the missionary has another idea. Look, she says, let me show you something. She takes some water and boils it. See, she says, there are spirits in the water, and when you put it on the fire they flee: those bubbles you see are the spirits escaping, the spirits that are making your children sick. Now boiling water makes sense. Now the babies stop dying. In belief, as in everything else, each of us must start from where we are.

When people get sick for unaccountable reasons in Manhattan, there is much talk of viruses and bacteria. Since doctors do not claim to be able to do much about most viruses, they do not put much effort into identifying them. Nor will the course of a viral infection be much changed by a visit to the doctor. In short, most appeals in everyday life to viruses are like most everyday appeals to witchcraft. They are supported only by a general conviction that sickness can be explained, and the conviction that viruses can make you sick.

If you ask most people in Manhattan why they believe in viruses, they will say two kinds of things: First, they will appeal to authority. "Science has shown," they will say, though if you ask them how science showed it, you will pretty quickly reach an impasse (even with scientists, by the way, unless they happen to be virologists unusually curious about the history of medicine). Second, they will point to phenomena—the spread of HIV or the common cold, the death of their great-aunt last winter, a picture of a virus they once saw in a magazine—where the viral theory explains what happened.

Similarly, in Kumasi, people who are asked why they believe in witchcraft will appeal to authority, too. "Our ancestors taught us about it." And they will then go on to tell you of cases of witch-craft they have seen or heard of, filling in for you all the things that it explains. Sir Edward Evans-Pritchard, one of the greatest anthro-pologists of the twentieth century, wrote a wonderful book called *Witchcraft, Oracles and Magic among the Azande*, about a people of that name who live in the Sudan. Having explained their ideas about witchcraft in great detail, he observes at one point that some-times, in the evenings, when he saw a flash of flame in the bush around the Azande settlement where he was living, he found him-self thinking, "Look, a witch." Of course, he didn't believe it, really. He knew it was probably someone from the village going off to relieve himself, carrying a flaming torch to guide him on his way. But what he was teaching us is that what you see depends on what you believe. What it's reasonable for you to think, faced with a par-ticular experience, depends on what ideas you already have.

Duhem's Discovery

That's as true of Western science as of traditional religion. In the early twentieth century, the French physicist Pierre Duhem noticed an interesting fact about the way scientists behave. When they do experiments or collect data to support their theories, other scien-tists, often those attached to different theories, deny that the evi-dence shows any such thing. The objections can be of many different kinds. They might say, for example, that the experiment really hasn't been done properly. (Your test tubes were contami-nated.) They might say that the so-called data are simply incor-rect. (We did the same experiment, and that's not what happened.) Or they could point out that their own theory explained the data just as well. (The theory that life on Earth arrived in the form of basic organisms on a meteorite explains the fossil data just as well as the theory that life evolved by the creation of its basic elements as a result of electrochemical processes in the primeval oceans.) Starting with this observation, he went on to propose a general claim that philosophers know as the Duhem thesis. However much data you have, Duhem said, there will be many theories that explain it equally well. Theories, to use the jargon, are underdetermined by the evidence.

For Positivism, the underdetermination of theory by evidence is a problem. If science is rational, then we want the process of scientific theorizing to give us reasons to believe the theories. And presumably we want to get the best theory we can, given the evidence. But if two people can always reasonably respond with different theories to the same evidence, then something other than reason or evidence must account for their choices. Furthermore, if this is true however much evidence we have, *there will always be more than one possible reasonable account of the facts*. And that will mean that no amount of scientific exploration will allow us to settle on a single picture of the way things are. If Positivism understates the place of reason in the justification of desires, and thus of values, it overstates the power of reason in the justification of belief, and thus of facts.

Underdetermination is worrying enough. But a later student of scientific thinking, the philosopher N. R. Hanson, noticed something equally troubling for the Positivist view about scientific thinking. The way the Positivists thought about getting evidence for our theories was this. First you collect the data; then you see what theories it supports. Observation and experiment, the collection of the basic facts, was supposed to be used as an independent support for theories. What Hanson noticed was that the data never came free of theoretical commitments. When Galileo said that he saw through the telescope that the moon had mountains, he was

assuming—as some of his opponents at the time pointed out—
that telescopes work just as well in space as on Earth. That happens to be right. But how did he know? No one, at that point, had
ever taken a telescope up into space to check. He just theorized that
it was so. And, in fact, it turns out to be enormously difficult—
Hanson thought it was literally impossible—to present data in language that isn't infused with theoretical ideas.

It doesn't matter for our purposes whether Hanson was right
about the impossibility of separating theory and data, because
what's certain is that we don't. When scientists looked at the tracks
of charged particles in photographs of cloud chambers—this was
the scientific example that Hanson knew best—they said things
like, "Look, there's the path of an electron." That's what was reasonable for them to believe. Yet for the rest of us, who don't know
the relevant physics or understand how the cloud chamber works,
it all looks just like a fuzzy line in a photograph. Hanson's insight
was that what it's reasonable for you to believe, as you look out on
the world, depends both on what you believe already and on what
ideas you have been introduced to. If you don't know about electricity—if you don't have the idea of it—you'll have no reason to
wonder, as Benjamin Franklin wondered, whether that is what
lightning is made of.

If what it's reasonable to believe depends on what you believe
already, however, then you can't check the reasonableness of all
your beliefs. You respond to new evidence in the light of what you
already believe, and that gives you new beliefs. Were the original
beliefs reasonable? Well, you can test them, but only by taking yet
other beliefs for granted. You can't get into the game of belief by
starting from nothing. And, of course, we all grow up in a family and
society that start us out with a great raft of beliefs that we could not
have developed on our own. Concepts and ideas develop in our
upbringing. Some concepts and ideas are based in our biological

natures—like color concepts, or the idea that there are physical objects in the world. But some ideas we wouldn't be using if we hadn't been given them—like electron, gene, democracy, contract, superego, witchcraft.

There is nothing unreasonable, then, about my kinsmen's belief in witchcraft. They think only what most people would think, given the concepts and beliefs they inherited; if you grew up with their beliefs and had their experiences, that is what you would believe, too. (Nor is belief in the agency of supernatural beings at all alien to the industrialized West: more than half of Americans believe in angels; roughly 40 percent think it's likely that Jesus will return to earth to render judgment sometime in the next half century.)

Those of us who were given scientific educations have a significant advantage. It's not that we are individually more reasonable; it's that we have been given better materials with which to think about the world. The institutions of science mean that the theories and ideas that scientists have developed are far superior to the ones that we human beings had before the growth of modern science. If we borrow their concepts, we are plugging ourselves into reality in ways that will make it easier for us to understand and to master the world. The best traditional predictors of the weather in Asante—and that is something that matters for a farming civilization—are simply not as good as the ones that the National Meteorological Office now provides, using modern scientific models. Who knows where we would be with the HIV/AIDS pandemic in Africa if we did not have modern scientific tools: tests for the virus, drugs for treatment, the understanding that predicts that condoms will prevent transmission of the disease? The advance of reason in the industrialized world is not the product of greater individual powers of reasoning. It is the result of the fact that we have developed institutions that can allow ordinary human beings to develop, test, and refine their ideas. What's wrong with the theory of witchcraft is not that it doesn't make sense but that it isn't true. And to find that out—in the way scientists gradually developed our modern understanding of disease—requires enormous, organized institutions of research, reflection, and analysis.

There is only one reality, and theories about witchcraft, like the germ theory of disease, are attempts to understand that one reality. Current medical theories of disease don't get everything right: otherwise, when you went to the doctor you could be guaranteed a diagnosis, a prognosis, perhaps even a cure. When an American gets a fever and assumes he has an infection, he's just doing what people have always done everywhere: he's applying the concepts that his culture has given him for thinking about disease. If, as I believe, this is a better story than a story about witchcraft, it's not because he's a better person. It's because he has the good fortune to live in a society that has spent enormous amounts of human resources to get that better story.

Scientific stories are not the only words we live by. I began with the ways our language of values helps guide us to a shared approach to the decisions that face us all. And one thing that is right in the Positivist picture is this: the methods of the natural sciences have not led to the kind of progress in our understanding of values that they have led to in our grasp of the facts. So we may be able to learn about values from societies where science is less deeply implanted than in ours: if scientific method has not advanced our understanding of values, then its superiority offers no reason to suppose that our understanding of values is superior. In fact, we have every reason to think that we can learn from other peoples, in ways both positive and negative. And if the Positivist asks *us* what guarantee we have that there is always going to be a way of persuading everyone of the value of everything valuable, we can ask *him* what guarantee he has that we can always persuade everyone of the facts. For the question presupposes that facts are in better shape than values here. And, even within the Positivist picture, as Duhem saw, there is no good reason to accept that claim.

That there are many ways of arguing for values of many kinds should be a good deal less puzzling when we recall that there are many kinds of facts for which we must offer different kinds of support, too. Mathematical beliefs can be justified by proofs. Beliefs about the colors of things get support from how they look in ordinary lighting. Psychological beliefs about other people get support from what they do and say. Beliefs about our own mental lives gain evidence, sometimes, from introspection. In the end, though, with facts as with values, nothing guarantees that we will be able to persuade everyone else of our view: this is a constraint that cosmopolitans, like everyone else, must accept. The Positivist holds that with facts, when we disagree, one of us has the truth, one of us is underwritten by the way things are, whereas with values, there is nothing to underwrite our claims. But even if we granted this picture, what would entitle us to think that the universe's being determinately one way or another guarantees that we can reach agreement as to which way it is? We enter every conversation—whether with neighbors or with strangers—without a promise of final agreement.

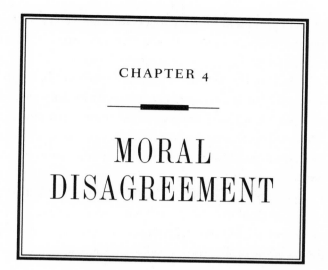

CHAPTER 4

MORAL DISAGREEMENT

Through Thick and Thin

You don't need to leave home to have disagreements about questions of value. In a crowd of people leaving a movie theater, someone thinks *Million Dollar Baby* superior to *Sideways*, but her companion demurs. "How can you respect a movie that tells you that the life of a quadriplegic is so worthless that you ought to kill her if she asks you to?" In a lively discussion after a barroom brawl, some say that the bystander who intervened was courageous, others that he was reckless and should just have called the cops. In a classroom discussion of abortion, one student says that first-trimester abortions are bad for the mother and the fetus, but that they ought to be legal, if the mother chooses. Another thinks that killing a fetus isn't even as bad as killing a grown-up cat. A third claims all abortion is murder. If we are to encourage cosmopolitan engagement, moral conversation between people *across* societies, we must expect such disagreements: after all, they occur *within* societies.

But moral conflicts come in different varieties. To begin with, our vocabulary of evaluation is enormously multifarious. Some terms—"good," "ought"—are, as philosophers often put it, rather *thin*. They express approval, but their application is otherwise pretty unconstrained: good soil, good dog, good argument, good idea, good person. Knowing what the word means doesn't tell you much about what it applies to. Of course, there are certain acts that you can't imagine thinking are good. That's because you can't make sense of approving of them, though not because it's somehow built into the meaning of the word "good" that, say, snatching food from a starving child doesn't count.

Much of our language of evaluation, however, is much "thicker" than this. To apply the concept of "rudeness," for example, you have to think of the act you're criticizing as a breach of good manners or as lacking the appropriate degree of concern for the feelings of others. I say, *"Thank you,"* ironically, when you accidentally step on my foot, implying that you did it deliberately. That's rude. Thanking a person, without irony, for something that he's done for you isn't. "Courage" is a term of praise. But its meaning is more substantive than a thin term like "right" or "good": to be courageous requires that you do something that strikes us as risky or dangerous, something where you have something to lose. Opening the front door could be courageous: but only if you had agoraphobia or knew that the secret police had rung the doorbell.

Thin concepts are something like placeholders. When notions of right and wrong are actually at work, they're thickly enmeshed in the complications of particular social contexts. In that sense, as the distinguished American political theorist Michael Walzer says, morality starts out thick. It's when you're trying to find points of agreement with others, say, that you start to abstract out the thin concepts that may underlie the thick ones.[1]

Thin concepts seem to be universal; we aren't the only people who have the concepts of right and wrong, good and bad; every society, it seems, has terms that correspond to these thin concepts, too. Even thick concepts like rudeness and courage are ones that you find pretty much everywhere. But there are thicker concepts still that really are peculiar to particular societies. And the most fundamental level of disagreement occurs when one party to a discussion invokes a concept that the other simply doesn't have. This is the kind of disagreement where the struggle is not to agree but just to understand.

Family Matters

Sometimes, familiar values are intertwined with unfamiliar customs and arrangements. People everywhere have ideas about your responsibility to your children, for instance. But who are your children? I grew up in two societies that conceived of family in rather different ways. In part, because these societies—Akan society in Ghana and the English world of my mother's kin—have been in touch with one another for several centuries, these differences are diminishing. Still, an important difference remains.

Consider the Akan idea of the *abusua*. This is a group of people related by common ancestry, who have relations of love and obligation to one another; the closer in time your shared ancestors, roughly speaking, the stronger the bonds. Sounds, in short, like a family. But there is an important difference between an *abusua* and a family. For your membership in an *abusua* depends only on who your mother is. Your father is irrelevant. If you are a woman, then your children are in your *abusua*, and so are the descendants of your daughters, and their daughters, on to the end of time. Membership in the *abusua* is shared like mitochondrial DNA, passing only through women. So I am in the same *abusua* as my sister's children but not in the same one as my brother's children. And, since I am not related to my father through a woman, he is not a member of my *abusua* either.

In short, the conception of the family in Akan culture is what anthropologists call *matrilineal*. A hundred years ago, in most lives, your mother's brother—your senior maternal uncle or *wɔfa*—would have played the role a father would have been expected to play in England. He was responsible, with the child's mother, for making sure that his sister's children—the word is *wɔfase*—were fed, clothed, and educated. Many married women lived with their brothers, visiting their husbands on a regular timetable. Of course, a man took an interest in his children, but his obligations to his children were relatively less demanding: rather like being an English uncle, in fact.

Visitors are often somewhat surprised that the word that you would most naturally use to refer to your brother or sister—which is *nua*—is also the word for the children of your mother's *sisters*. And, in fact, people sometimes will tell you, in Ghanaian English, that someone is "my sister, same father, same mother," which you might have thought was a couple of qualifications too many. (If someone tells you that a woman is his junior mother, on the other hand, he's referring to his mother's younger sister.)

When I was a child all this was changing. More men were living with their wives and children and not supporting their sisters' children. But my father still got the school reports of his sister's children, sent them pocket money, discussed, with their mothers, their schooling, paid the bills at the family house of his *abusua*. He also regularly ate with his favorite sister, while his children and wife—that's us—ate together at home.

There are, in short, different ways of organizing family life. Which one makes sense to you will depend, in good measure, on the concepts with which you grew up. As long as a society has a way of assigning responsibilities for the nurture of children that works and makes sense, it seems to me, it would be odd to say that one way was the right way of doing it, and all the others wrong. We feel, rightly, that a father who is delinquent in his child support payments is doing something wrong. Many Asante, especially in the past, would feel the same about a delinquent *wɔfa*. Once you understand the system, you'll be likely to agree: and it won't be because you've given up any of your basic moral commitments. There are thin, universal values here—those of good parenting—but their expression is highly particular, thickly enmeshed with local customs and expectations and the facts of social arrangements.

Red Peppers on Wednesdays

But there are other local values that scarcely correspond to anything you might recognize as important. My father, for example, wouldn't eat "bush meat," animals killed in the forest. This included venison, and, he used to tell us, when he once ate it by accident in England, his skin broke out in a rash the next day. Had you asked him why he wouldn't eat bush meat, though, he wouldn't have said he didn't like it or that he was allergic to it. He would have told you—if he thought it was any of your business—that it was *akyiwadee* for him, because he was of the clan of the Bush Cow. Etymologically *akyiwadee* means something like "a thing you turn your back on," and, if you had to guess at the translation of it, you would presumably suggest "taboo." That is, of course, a word that came into English from a Polynesian language, where it was used to refer to a class of things that people of certain groups strenuously avoided.

As in Polynesia, in Asante doing one of these forbidden things leaves you "polluted," and there are various remedies, ways of "cleansing" yourself. We all have experience with the sense of revulsion, and the desire to cleanse ourselves, but that doesn't mean that we really have the concept of *akyiwadeɛ*. Because to have that idea—that thick concept—you have to think that there are things that you ought not to do because of your clan membership, or because they are taboo to a god to whom you owe allegiance. Now, you might say that there's a rationale of sorts for a member of the Bush Cow clan's not eating bush meat. Your clan animal is, symbolically, a relative of yours; so, for you, eating it (and its relatives) is a bit like eating a person. And perhaps this is one rationalization that a member of the clan might offer. But the list of *akyiwadeɛ* in traditional Asante society far exceeds anything that you can make sense of in this sort of way. One shrine god named Edinkra— mentioned in the 1920s by Captain Rattray, the colonial anthropologist who first wrote extensively about Asante traditions—had among its taboos red peppers on Wednesdays.

Now, I don't claim that you can't learn what *akyiwadeɛ* means: indeed, I hope you pretty much grasp how the word is used on the basis of what I've told you already, and if you read the complete works of Captain Rattray, you'd know a lot more about Akan taboos, certainly enough to grasp the concept. Nevertheless, this isn't an idea that plays any role in your actual thinking. There are acts we avoid that we rather loosely call "taboo," of course: the prohibition on incest, for example. But you don't really think incest is to be avoided because it is taboo. Your thought is exactly the other way round: it's "taboo" because there are good reasons not to do it.

Some *akyiwadeɛ*, like the one that prohibited my father from eating venison, are specific to particular kinds of people, as is evidenced in a proverb that makes a metaphor of the fact:

> Nnipa gu ahodoɔ mmiɛnsa, nanso obiara wɔ n'akyiwadeɛ:
> ɔhene, ɔdehyeɛ na akoa. Ɔhene akyiwadeɛ ne akyinnyeɛ, ɔdehyeɛ
> deɛ ne nsamu, na akoa deɛ ne nkyeraseɛ.
>
> *People fall into three kinds, but everyone has his own taboo: the*
> *ruler, the royal, and the slave. The ruler's taboo is disagreement, the*
> *royal's is disrespect, and the slave's is the revealing of origins.*

As a result, even if you were in Asante, many taboos wouldn't affect you, since you don't belong to an Asante clan and don't have obligations to shrine gods. But there are many things all Asantes "turn their backs on" and would expect everyone else to as well. Given that some of them have to do with contact with menstruating women or men who have recently had sex, they can affect strangers, even if strangers don't act on them. Once you know about the taboos, they can raise questions as to how you should act. Since, for example, shaking hands with a menstruating woman is taboo to a chief, some visitors to the Asante court have a decision to make about whether to come to a meeting.

I have deliberately not used the word "moral" to describe these taboos. They are certainly values: they guide acts, thoughts, and feelings. They are unlike what we would think of as moral values, however, in at least three ways. First, they don't always apply to everybody. Only members of the Ekuona clan have the obligation to avoid bush meat. Second, you are polluted if you break a taboo, even if you do it by accident. So, whereas with an offense against morality, "I didn't mean to do it" counts as a substantial defense, with taboo breaking, the reply must be, "It doesn't matter what you meant to do. You're polluted. You need to get clean." Oedipus was no better off for having broken the incest taboo unknowingly. A final difference between taboos and moral demands is that breaches of them pollute mostly *you:* they aren't fundamentally about how you should treat other people; they're about how you should keep yourself (ritually) clean.

Now, all around the world many people have believed in something like *akyiwadeε,* and the analogous term, *tabu* or whatever, is certainly a powerful part of evaluative language. But—at least nowadays—while the avoidance of taboos is still important to people, it isn't as important as many other sorts of values. That's partly because, as I said, while breaches of taboo produce pollution, that pollution can usually be ritually cleansed. The laws of kashrut for Orthodox Jews in our country are like this, too: obedience to them is important, and so is a commitment to obeying them if you can. If you break them accidentally, however, the right response is not guilt but the appropriate ritual form of purification. Moral offenses—theft, assault, murder—on the other hand, are not expiated by purification. Now there are historical trends that help explain why a concern with *akyiwadeε* plays a smaller part in contemporary life in my hometown than it would have done when my father was growing up. One reason is that even more people now are Christian and Muslim, and these taboos are associated with earlier forms of religion. Our earlier religious ideas survive, as I've noted, even in the lives of devout believers in these global faiths. They just have less weight than they had before they were competing with Jehovah and Allah. In the old days, you had reason to fear the wrath of the gods or the ancestors if you broke taboos— that was part of why it was important to make peace with them by cleansing yourself. But these powers have less respect in the contemporary world. (When my Christian sister wanted to protect us from witchcraft, you'll recall, she went to a Muslim.)

Another reason is that the forms of identity—the clan identities, for example—with which they are often associated are just a good deal less significant than they used to be. People still mostly know their clans. And in the past, when you showed up in a strange town in another part of the Akan world, you could have sought hospitality from the local leaders of your clan. Now, however, there are hotels; travel is commoner (so the demands of clan hospitality could easily become oppressive); and clans, like the families of which they are a part, recede in importance anyway when so many people live away from the places where they were born.

Equally important, I think, most people in Kumasi know now that our taboos are local: that strangers do not know what is and is not taboo and that, if they do, they have taboos of their own. So increasingly people think of taboos as "things *we* don't do." The step from "what *we* don't do" to "what we *happen* not to do" can be a small one; and then people can come to think of these practices as the sort of quaint local custom that one observes without much enthusiasm and, in the end, only when it doesn't cause too much fuss.

Gross Points

The *akyiwadeε* is, as we've seen, thickly enmeshed in all sorts of customs and factual beliefs (not least the existence of irascible ancestors and shrine gods), and one response to such alien values is just to dismiss them as primitive and irrational. But if that is what they are, then the primitive and the irrational are pervasive here, too. Indeed, the affect, the sense of repugnance, that underlies *akyiwadeε* is surely universal: that's one reason it's not difficult to grasp. Many Americans eat pigs but won't eat cats. It would be hard to make the case that cats are, say, dirtier or more intelligent than pigs. And since there are societies where people *will* eat cats, we know that it is possible for human beings to eat them with pleasure and without danger. Most American meat eaters who refuse to eat cats have only the defense that the very thought of it fills them with disgust. Indeed, all of us have things that we find contact with polluting: touching them makes us feel dirty; eating them would nauseate us. We're likely to run off to wash our hands or wash out our mouths if we come into contact with them. Mostly, when we have these responses, we defend them as rational: cockroaches and rats and other people's saliva or vomit do actually carry diseases, we say; cats and dogs taste horrible. Yet these reactions are not really explained by the stories we tell. Flies carry most of the same risks as cockroaches, but usually produce less "pollution." And people are disgusted by the idea of drinking orange juice that has had a cockroach in it, even if they know that the cockroach was rigorously cleansed of all bacteria by being autoclaved in advance. They're reluctant to eat chocolate shaped like dog feces, even if they know exactly what it is.

Psychologists (notably Paul Rozin, who has conducted many experiments along these lines) think that this capacity for disgust is a fundamental human trait, one that evolved in us because distinguishing between what you will and will not eat is an important cognitive task for an omnivorous species like our own. Disgust goes with nausea, because it is a response that developed to deal with food that we should avoid. But that capacity for disgust, like all our natural capacities, can be built on by culture. Is it the *same* capacity that makes some men in many cultures feel polluted when they learn they have shaken hands with a menstruating woman? Or that makes most Americans squirm in disgust at the thought of incest? I don't think we yet know. The pervasiveness of these taboo responses does suggest, however, that they draw on something deep in human nature.[2]

Most people in this country, both secular and religious, think that the attitudes of some of their contemporaries to certain sexual acts—masturbation and homosexuality, for instance, or even consensual adult incest—are simply versions of taboos found in many cultures around the world. In the so-called Holiness Code, at the end of Leviticus, for example, eating animals that have died of natural causes requires you to wash yourself and your clothes, and even then you will be unclean until the evening (Leviticus 17:15–16). Priests, "the sons of Aaron," are told at Leviticus 22:5–8 that if they touch people or "any swarming thing" that is polluting, they must bathe and wait until sunset before they can eat the "sacred donations." The same chapters proscribe the consuming of blood, bodily self-mutilation (tattoos, shaving for priests, cutting gashes in one's flesh, though not, of course, male circumcision), and seeing various of one's relatives naked, while prescribing detailed rules for certain kinds of sacrifice. For most modern Christians, these regulations are parts of Jewish law that Christ freed people from. But the famous proscriptions of a man's "lying with a man as with a woman" are to be found alongside these passages, along with commands to avoid incest and bestiality, which most Christians still endorse.[3]

Earlier in Leviticus, we find an extensive set of proscriptions on contact, both direct and indirect, with menstruating women and rules for cleansing oneself from that form of pollution; as well as rules that indicate that male ejaculation is polluting, so that, even after a man has bathed, he is ritually unclean until evening.[4] Like Akan traditions, these rules are embedded in metaphysical beliefs: they are repeatedly said to be laws given by God to Moses for the Israelites, and often they have religious explanations embedded in them. The prohibition on consuming blood is explained thus:

> For the life of the flesh is in the blood. And as for Me, I have given
> it to you on the altar to ransom your lives, for it is the blood that

ransoms in exchange for life. Therefore have I said to the Israelites: no living person among you shall consume blood, nor shall the sojourner who sojourns in your midst consume blood.[5]

Leviticus should remind us that appeals to values do not come neatly parceled out according to kinds. You might think that failing to respect your parents is a bad thing, but that it's bad in a way that's different from adultery; different, too, from sex with an animal; different, again, from incest with your daughter-in-law. I confess that I do not think sex between men, even if they lie with one another "as with a woman," is bad at all. But all of these acts are proscribed in succession by the Holiness Code; in fact (in Leviticus 20:9–13) all of them are deemed worthy of death.

Among those who take them seriously, these prohibitions evoke a deep, visceral response; they're also entangled in beliefs about metaphysical or religious matters. The combination of these two features is what makes them so difficult to discuss with people who share neither the response nor the metaphysics. Yet even with values we do not take seriously, there is something to be hoped for: namely, understanding. Nor do you have to share a value to feel how it might motivate someone. We can be moved by Antigone's resolve to bury her brother's corpse, even if (unlike those Indians and Greeks that Darius scandalized) we couldn't care less about how cadavers are disposed of, and think she shouldn't really, either.

And while taboos can lead to genuine disagreements about what to do, many people readily understand that such values vary from place to place. Asante people largely accept now that others don't feel the power of our taboos; we know that they may have their own. And, most importantly, these local values do not, of course, stop us from also recognizing, as we do, kindness, generosity, and compassion, or cruelty, stinginess, and inconsiderateness—virtues and vices that are recognized widely among human societies.

So, too, scattered among the various abominations in Leviticus we come across, from time to time, appeals to values that are universal and that discipline the demands made by the taboos. Leviticus 19 commands us to leave a share of our crops for the poor, to avoid lying and dissembling, fraud, and theft; not to speak ill of the deaf or put a stumbling block in the way of the blind; not to slander our relatives. Indeed, it makes the impossibly demanding command that "you shall love your fellow man as yourself" (Leviticus 19:18). There are values here that not all of us recognize; there are many we all do.

Terms of Contention

Cosmopolitans suppose that all cultures have enough overlap in their vocabulary of values to begin a conversation. But they don't suppose, like some universalists, that we could all come to agreement if only we had the same vocabulary. Despite what they say in Japan, almost every American knows what it is to be polite, a thickish concept. That doesn't mean that we can't disagree about when politeness is on display. A journalist interviews a foreign dictator, someone who is known for his abuses of human rights. She speaks deferentially, frequently calling him Your Excellency. She says, "Some people have suggested that you have political prisoners in your jails," when everybody knows that this is so. "What do you say, Your Excellency, to the accusations of torture by your secret police?" "Nonsense," he replies. "Lies made up by people who want to confuse foreigners about the progress we are making in my country." She moves on. Is this politeness? Or is it a craven abdication of the journalist's obligation to press for the truth? Can it be both? If it is politeness, is it appropriate, in these circumstances, to be polite? You can imagine such a conversation proceeding for a long while without resolution.

Politeness is a value term from the repertory of manners, which we usually take to be less serious than morals. But this sort of controversy also surrounds the application of more straightforwardly ethical terms—like "brave"—and more centrally moral ones—like "cruel." Like most terms for virtues and vices, "courage" and "cruelty" are what philosophers call "open-textured": two people who both know what they mean can reasonably disagree about whether they apply in a particular case.[6] Grasping what the words mean doesn't give you a rule that will definitively decide whether it applies in every case that might come along. Nearly half a century ago, the philosopher of law H. L. A. Hart offered as an example of open texture, a bylaw that prohibits "vehicles" in a public park. Does it apply to a two-inch-long toy car in a child's pocket? "Vehicle" has an open texture. There are things to be said on either side. Of course, in the context of the rule, it may be clear that the idea was to stop people from driving around, disturbing the peace. Let the child bring in the toy. But doesn't that rationale suggest that a skateboard is a vehicle? There need be no reason to think that those who made the rule had any answer to this question in mind. Our language works very well in ordinary and familiar cases. Once things get interesting, even people who know the language equally well can disagree.

The open texture of our evaluative language is even more obvious. One of my great-uncles once led a cavalry charge against a machine-gun emplacement, armed with a sword. Brave? Or just foolhardy? (You may have guessed that this uncle was Asante; actually, he was English, fighting against the Ottomans in the First World War. Great-Uncle Fred called his autobiography *Life's a Gamble*, so you can tell he was willing to take risks.) Aristotle argued that courage involved an *intelligent* response to danger, not just ignoring it. Perhaps, in the circumstances and given his aims, that saber charge *was* the smartest thing to do. Still, even if we got as full a story as we could ask for about the exact circumstances, you and I might end up disagreeing.

Several years ago, an international parliament of religious leaders issued what they called a "universal declaration of a global ethic." The credo's exhortations had the quality of those horoscopes that seem wonderfully precise while being vague enough to suit all comers. "We must not commit any kind of sexual immorality": a fine sentiment, unless we don't agree about what counts as sexual immorality. "We must put behind us all forms of domination and abuse": but societies that, by our lights, subject women to domination and abuse are unlikely to recognize themselves in that description. They're convinced that they're protecting women's honor and chastity. "We must strive for a just social and economic order, in which everyone has an equal chance to reach full potential as a human being": a Randian will take this to be an endorsement of unfettered capitalism, as a Fabian will take it to be an endorsement of socialism.

And so it goes with our most central values. Is it cruel to kill cattle in slaughterhouses where live cattle can smell the blood of the dead? Or to spank children in order to teach them how to behave? The point is not that we couldn't argue our way to one position or the other on these questions; it's only to say that when we disagree, it won't always be because one of us just doesn't understand the value that's at stake. It's because applying value terms to new cases requires judgment and discretion. Indeed, it's often part of our understanding of these terms that their applications are *meant* to be argued about. They are, to use another piece of philosopher's jargon, *essentially contestable*. For many concepts, as W. B. Gallie wrote in introducing the term, "proper use inevitably involves endless disputes about their proper use on the part of users."[7] Evaluative language, I've been insisting, aims to shape not just our acts but our thoughts and our feelings. When we describe past acts with words like "courageous" and "cowardly," "cruel" and "kind," we are shaping what people think and feel about what was done—and shaping our understanding of our moral language as well. Because that language is open-textured and essentially contestable, even people who share a moral vocabulary have plenty to fight about.

Fool's Gold

Consider even the "Golden Rule," which the leaders of the Parliament of the World's Religions agreed was the "fundamental principle" on which the global ethic was based: "What you do not wish done to yourself, do not do to others," or in positive terms, "What you wish done to yourself, do to others." Since it is, indeed, the most obvious candidate for a global ethical idea, it is worth, I think, explaining briefly why it doesn't cut much ice. As we see, the rule famously has two nonequivalent versions. Sometimes, in its more modest and negative version, it urges us not to do unto others what we wouldn't have done to us; sometimes, in more demanding and positive tones, it commands that we must do to others what we would like done to ourselves. Still, either way, it embodies an attractive idea: when you're doing things to people, imagine how the world looks from their point of view. And the basic moral sentiment is widespread. "Do not do to others what you do not want them to do to you": that's from Confucius's *Analects* 15:23. "This is the sum of duty: do nothing to others that would cause you pain if done to you": that's from the *Mahabharata* 5:1517. "Therefore all things whatsoever ye would that men should do to

you, do ye even so to them: for this is the law and the prophets":
that's from the King James Bible, Matthew 7:12. But even though
some version or other of the rule has broad scriptural sanction, the
Golden Rule is not as helpful as it might at first seem.

To see why, notice first that when you do something to someone, what you do can be truly described in infinitely many ways.
When it's described in some of those ways, the person you did it
to may be glad you did it; when it's described in other ways, he
may not. Suppose you're a doctor considering saving the life of a
Jehovah's Witness by giving her a blood transfusion. What you
want to do is: save her life. That, of course, is exactly what you
would want done unto you, if your medical situation was the same
as hers. It is also, we may suppose, what she wants done unto her.
But you also want to do this: give her a blood transfusion. That,
too, is what you would want done to you. Unfortunately, it is not
what your patient wants. Most Witnesses, you see, interpret
Leviticus 3:17—which says, "An everlasting statue for your generations in all your dwelling places, no fat and no blood shall you
eat"—as prohibiting blood transfusions. Since obeying the Lord's
commands is more important to her than this earthly life, under
this description she's vehemently opposed to what you want to do.
She'd literally rather be dead. The first problem with the Golden
Rule, in any of its versions, in practice, is that to apply it I have to
know not just why I am doing what I am doing unto others—the
description of the act that matters to me—but also how the act
will strike those others.

So what should you do? Your first thought might be that you
would be perfectly happy to have the blood transfusion if you were
in her situation. Taken that way, the Golden Rule says, "Go ahead."
But what's her situation? Is it the situation of someone about to
die unless she gets a blood transfusion, or the situation of someone whose life can be saved only by disobeying God's command-

ments? If I thought that I was going to go to hell if you gave me a blood transfusion, I wouldn't want it either. Once you look at it that way, the Golden Rule pushes you in the other direction. So, when I think about what I should do unto others, is what matters whether I'd like it done to me with my actual values and beliefs, or is what matters whether I'd like it done to me if I had their values and beliefs?

Unfortunately, I think the answer is: neither. Suppose the blood came from an African American and your patient was a racist—are you supposed to ask what you would like done to you if you were a racist? Somehow, I can't imagine that's what Confucius or Jesus had in mind. But it's not just the fact that racism is mistaken that makes the difference. I think that the Witness's interpretation of Leviticus is wrong. Leviticus 3 is clearly about eating meat that has been prepared for sacrifice to God; verse 17 is underlining the point that the fat should be burned and the blood should have been cast around the altar. In context, I think it's clear that putting blood that is the free gift of another person into your veins in order to save your life just isn't "eating blood." Nevertheless, I still think the fact that she doesn't want the blood is important, even though it wouldn't be important to me.

I don't have a clear answer as to why this is so. Sometimes, when I'm asking, as I think one often should, "How would I like it if they did that to me?," I imagine myself sharing the beliefs and values of the other person; but sometimes I don't. Suppose my patient thinks that Canadian drugs are inferior to American ones. He's not crazy. There's been an organized campaign, directed by apparently responsible people, to persuade him of this. I can give him one of two pills, one cheap and Canadian, one expensive and made in the USA. I am completely confident that their medical effects are equivalent. Should I offer him a choice? I'm not sure. But it won't help to ask what I would want done to me in those circumstances, unless I know whether the circumstances include having this mistaken belief.

These problems are part of a general difficulty. Immanuel Kant argued that whenever you were trying to pick the right thing to do, you should identify a universal principle on which to act (he called it a "maxim"), and then ask, roughly, whether you would be happy if everyone had to act on that maxim. So he thought, for example, that you shouldn't break your promises just because it suits you, because you couldn't want everybody to do this; if all did, no one would believe you when you made a promise. This is called "universalizing" the maxim. But it can be very hard to identify what maxim you are acting on, especially given that, as I shall argue in the next chapter, it is often much clearer to us *what* we should do than *why*.

The idea behind the Golden Rule is that we should take other people's interests seriously, take them into account. It suggests that we learn about other people's situations, and then use our imaginations to walk a while in their moccasins. These are aims we cosmopolitans endorse. It's just that we can't claim that the way is easy.

Which Values Matter Most?

There is yet a third way of disagreeing about values. Even if we share a value language, and even if we agree on how to apply it to a particular case, we can disagree about the weight to give to different values. Confucius, for example, in the *Analects*, recommends that a son respect his parents. A *chün tzu* (or, as it is often translated, "a gentleman") should be generous to those who have done well by him and avoid vindictiveness to those who have done him injury; he should avoid avarice and not let self-interest get in the way of doing what is right. He should be courageous, wise, keep his word. Summarized in this, no doubt, simplistic way, Confucius can sound uncannily like Polonius (and equally banal). But the fact that we share these values with him doesn't mean that we will always agree with him about what we ought to think and feel. Confucius placed a great deal more weight on obedience to authority, for example, than most of us would. The result is that sometimes Confucius would clearly respond to the demands of the many values we both recognize in ways different from us. We may all agree that it would be better, if we can, not to marry a spouse our parents dislike, but most Westerners also think that love could justifiably lead us to disobey them if they tried to get in the way of our marrying the man or woman of our dreams. In the magical second scene of Act II of *Romeo and Juliet*, Juliet represents the issue as one of giving up names: she wants Romeo to "deny thy father and refuse his name"; she offers that she will "no longer be a Capulet."

> 'Tis but thy name that is my enemy;
> Thou art thyself, though not a Montague.
> . . . Romeo, doff thy name,
> And for thy name which is no part of thee
> Take all myself.

Confucius would surely respond that Juliet, in speaking of their connection to their families as if it were a matter of mere convention—just names, idle words—covers up the fact that she wants to tear the most powerful natural moral bond, the tie that binds parents irrevocably to their children.

But such conflicts among shared values can take place within a single society—indeed, within a single human heart. Hegel famously said that tragedy involved the clash not between good and evil but between two goods. Agamemnon, as commander of the Greek army, had to choose between the interests of the Trojan expedition and his devotion to his wife and daughter. Such dilemmas are a mainstay of imaginative fiction, but clashes among our own values, if usually less exalted, are an everyday occurrence.

Most people will agree that there is something *unfair* about punishing people for doing something that they couldn't have been expected to know was wrong. Many tax laws are extremely hard to understand; even after taking good advice from a reputable accountant, you can end up in trouble. If you haven't paid enough tax as a result, you'll be charged a penalty. Surely that's unfair, according to the principle I just enunciated. The question is whether it's unfair enough to change the law. People can disagree. After all, there's something to be said for keeping down the costs of enforcing the tax laws. Efficiency, in short, is a value, too. And if you had a rule that said that you wouldn't be charged a penalty if you had made a good faith effort to apply the tax laws as you understood them, then the courts would be full of people trying to prove that they'd made such a good faith effort. You'd probably even tempt some people to *pretend* they'd made a good faith effort, thus creating a new moral hazard in our tax laws. Disputes about whether tax laws are just can get quite contentious in America; but there are even more serious cases where values come into conflict.

Take criminal punishment. No reasonable person thinks that it's a good thing to punish innocent people. But we all know that human institutions are imperfect, that our knowledge is always fallible, and that juries are not free from prejudice. So we know that sometimes innocent people will be punished. That would seem like an argument for abandoning criminal punishment; but, of course, we also think that it's important to punish the guilty, not least because we fear that there'd be a lot more crime if we didn't. Here again, we may be unable to agree on how to strike the balance between avoiding the injustice of punishing the innocent and other values, even though we agree on what other values are at stake: security of people and property, justice, retribution . . . there's a long list. This is one source of disagreement about capital punishment. The legal scholar Charles Black argued that "caprice and mistake" are inevitable in capital trials and that killing an innocent person was too important a mistake to risk.[8] Many proponents of capital punishment believe it's important to punish those who deserve to die; important enough, in fact, that we must, regretfully, accept that we will sometimes do this great wrong. Not to do the right thing in the cases where we punish the guilty, they think, would be a greater wrong. So you can find people on either side of the capital-punishment debate who share the same values, but weight them differently.

Disputing with Strangers

We've identified three kinds of disagreement about values: we can fail to share a vocabulary of evaluation; we can give the same vocabulary different interpretations; and we can give the same values different weights. Each of these problems seems more likely to arise if the discussion involves people from different societies. Mostly we share evaluative language with our neighbors, you might think. And while evaluation is essentially contestable, the range of disagreement will usually be wider—will it not?—when people from different places are trying to come to a shared evaluation. Maybe you and I won't always agree about what's polite. Still, at least its *politeness* we're disagreeing about. Other societies will have words that behave roughly like our word "polite" and will have something like the idea of "good manners," but an extra level of difference will arise from the fact that this thick vocabulary of evaluation is embedded in different ways of life. And, finally, we know that one way in which societies differ is in the relative weight they put on different values.

In the Arab world, and in much of Central and South Asia, there are societies in which men believe that their honor is tied up with the chastity of their sisters, their daughters, and their wives. Now, men here, too, feel shamed, dishonored, when their wives or daughters are raped. But, unless they come from one of those honor-based societies, they aren't likely to think that the solution is to punish these women. We understand the reflected glory of the achievements of our relatives, and we know that with the possibility of pride comes the option of shame. Yet family honor is not as important to us now as it clearly is, and was, to others. So you might conclude that cross-cultural conversations about values are bound to end in disagreement; indeed, you might fear that they would inflame conflict rather than creating understanding.

There are three problems with this conclusion. First, we can agree about *what* to do even when we don't agree *why*. Second, we exaggerate the role of reasoned argument in reaching or failing to reach agreements about values. And, third, most conflicts don't arise from warring values in the first place. I'll defend these claims in the next chapter.

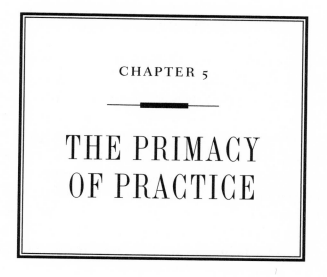

CHAPTER 5

THE PRIMACY
OF PRACTICE

Local Agreements

Among the Asante, you will be glad to hear, incest between brothers and sisters and parents and children is shunned as *akyiwadeε*. You can agree with an Asante that it's wrong, even if you don't accept his explanation of why. If my interest is in discouraging theft, I needn't worry that one person might refrain from theft because she believes in the Golden Rule; another because of her conception of personal integrity; a third because she thinks God frowns on it. I've said that value language helps shape common responses of thought, action, and feeling. But when the issue is what to do, differences in what we think and feel can fall away. We know from our own family lives that conversation doesn't start with agreement on principles. Who but someone in the grip of a terrible theory would want to insist on an agreement on principles

— 69 —

before discussing which movie to go to, what to have for dinner, when to go to bed?

Indeed, our political coexistence, as subjects or citizens, depends on being able to agree about practices while disagreeing about their justification. For many long years, in medieval Spain under the Moors and later in the Ottoman Near East, Jews and Christians of various denominations lived under Muslim rule. This modus vivendi was possible only because the various communities did not have to agree on a set of universal values. In seventeenth-century Holland, starting roughly in the time of Rembrandt, the Sephardic Jewish community began to be increasingly well integrated into Dutch society, and there was a great deal of intellectual as well as social exchange between Christian and Jewish communities. Christian toleration of Jews did not depend on express agreement on fundamental values. Indeed, these historical examples of religious toleration—you might even call them early experiments in multiculturalism—should remind us of the most obvious fact about our own society.

Americans share a willingness to be governed by the system set out in the U. S. Constitution. But that does not require anyone to agree to any particular claims or values. The Bill of Rights tells us, "Congress shall make no law respecting an establishment of religion, or prohibiting the free exercise thereof. . . ." Yet we don't need to agree on what values underlie our acceptance of the First Amendment's treatment of religion. Is it religious toleration as an end in itself? Or is it a Protestant commitment to the sovereignty of the individual conscience? Is it prudence, which recognizes that trying to force religious conformity on people only leads to civil discord? Or is it skepticism that any religion has it right? Is it to protect the government from religion? Or religion from the government? Or is it some combination of these, or other, aims?

Cass Sunstein, the American legal scholar, has written eloquently that our understanding of Constitutional law is a set of what he calls "incompletely theorized agreements."[1] People mostly agree that it would be wrong for the Congress to pass laws prohibiting the building of mosques, for example, without agreeing exactly as to why. Many of us would, no doubt, mention the First Amendment (even though we don't agree about what values it embodies). But others would ground their judgment not in any particular law but in a conception, say, of democracy or in the equal citizenship of Muslims, neither of which is explicitly mentioned in the Constitution. There is no agreed-upon answer—and the point is there doesn't need to be. We can live together without agreeing on what the values are that make it good to live together; we can agree about what to do in most cases, without agreeing about why it is right.

I don't want to overstate the claim. No doubt there are widely shared values that help Americans live together in amity. But they certainly don't live together successfully because they have a shared theory of value or a shared story as to how to bring "their" values to bear in each case. They each have a pattern of life that they are used to; and neighbors who are, by and large, used to them. So long as this settled pattern is not seriously disrupted, they do not worry over-much about whether their fellow citizens agree with them or their theories about how to live. Americans tend to have, in sum, a broadly liberal reaction when they *do* hear about their fellow citizens' doing something that they would not do themselves: they mostly think it is not their business and not the government's business either. And, as a general rule, their shared American-ness matters to them, although many of their fellow Americans are remarkably unlike themselves. It's just that what they do share can be less substantial than we're inclined to suppose.

Changing Our Minds

It's not surprising, then, that what makes conversation across boundaries worthwhile isn't that we're likely to come to a reasoned agreement about values. I don't say that we can't change minds, but the reasons we exchange in our conversations will seldom do much to persuade others who do not share our fundamental evaluative judgments already. (Remember: the same goes, mutatis mutandis, for factual judgments.)

When we offer judgments, after all, it's rarely because we have applied well-thought-out principles to a set of facts and deduced an answer. Our efforts to justify what we have done—or what we plan to do—are typically made up after the event, rationalizations of what we have decided intuitively. And a good deal of what we intuitively take to be right, we take to be right just because it is what we are used to. If you live in a society where children are spanked, you will probably spank your children. You will believe that it is a good way to teach them right from wrong and that, despite the temporary suffering caused by a beating, they will end up better off for it. You will point to the wayward child and say, sotto voce, that his parents do not know how to discipline him; you will mean that they do not beat him enough. You will also, no doubt, recognize that there are people who beat their children too hard or too often. So you will recognize that beating a child can sometimes be cruel.

Much the same can be said about the practice of female genital cutting, to return to a previous example. If you've grown up taking it for granted as the normal thing to do, you will probably respond at first with surprise to someone who thinks it is wrong. You will offer reasons for doing it—that unmodified sexual organs are unaesthetic; that the ritual gives young people the opportunity to display courage in their transition to adulthood; that you can see their excitement as they go to their ceremony, their pride when they return. You will say that it is very strange that someone who has not been through it should presume to know whether or not sex is pleasurable for you. And, if someone should try to force you to stop from the outside, you may decide to defend the practice as an expression of your cultural identity. But this is likely to be as much a rationalization as are the arguments of your critics. They say it is mutilation, but is that any more than a reflex response to an unfamiliar practice? They exaggerate the medical risks. They say that female circumcision demeans women, but do not seem to think that male circumcision demeans men.

I am not endorsing these claims, or celebrating the argumentative impasse, or, indeed, the poverty of reason in much discussion within and across cultures. But let's recognize this simple fact: a large part of what we do we do because it *is* just what we do. You get up in the morning at eight-thirty. Why *that* time? You have coffee and cereal. Why not porridge? You send the kids to school. Why not teach them at home? You have to work. Why that job, though? Reasoning—by which I mean the public act of exchanging stated justifications—comes in not when we are going on in the usual way, but when we are thinking about change. And when it comes to change, what moves people is often not an argument from a principle, not a long discussion about values, but just a gradually acquired new way of seeing things.

My father, for example, came from a society in which neither women nor men were traditionally circumcised. Indeed, circumcision was *akyiwadeε;* and since chiefs were supposed to be unblemished, circumcision was a barrier to holding royal office. Nevertheless, as he tells us in his autobiography, he decided as a teenager to have himself circumcised.

As was the custom in those happy days, the young girls of Adum would gather together in a playing field nearby on moonlight nights to regale themselves by singing traditional songs and dancing from about 7 PM until midnight each day of the week.

. . . On one such night, these girls suddenly started a new song that completely bowled us over: not only were the words profane in the extreme, but they also constituted the most daring challenge to our manhood and courage ever flung at us. More than that, we were being invited to violate an age-old tradition of our ancestors, long respected among our people, namely the taboo on circumcision. Literally translated the words were:

"An uncircumcised penis is detestable, and those who are uncircumcised should come for money from us so that they can get circumcised. We shall never marry the uncircumcised."[2]

To begin with, my father and his friends thought the girls would relent. But they were wrong. And so, after consultation with his mates, my father found himself a *wansam*—a Muslim circumcision specialist—and had the operation performed. (It was, he said, the most painful experience of his life and, if he'd had it to do again, he would have refrained. He did not, of course, have the advantage of the preparation, the companionship of boys of his own age, and the prestige of suffering bravely that would have come if the practice had been an Akan tradition.)

My father offered a reason for this decision: he and his friends conceded that "as our future sweethearts and wives, they were entitled to be heard in their plea in favor of male circumcision, even though they were not prepared to go in for female circumcision, which was also a taboo among our people." This explanation invites a question, however. Why did these young women, in the heart of Asante, decide to urge the young men of Adum to do what was not just untraditional but taboo? One possibility is that circumcision somehow became identified in their minds with being modern. If that was the point, my father would have been sympathetic. He was traditional in some ways; but like many people in Kumasi in the early twentieth century, he was also excited by a modern world that was bringing new music, new technology, new possibilities. To volunteer for circumcision in his society he surely had not just to hear the plea of the young women of Adum but to understand—and agree with—the impulse behind it. And, as I say, it may have been exactly the fact that it was untraditional that made it appealing. Circumcision—especially because it carried with it exclusion from the possibilities of traditional political office— became a way of casting his lot with modernity.

This new fashion among the young people of Adum was analogous to, if more substantial than, the change in taste that has produced a generation of Americans with piercings and tattoos. And that change was not simply the result of argument and debate, either (even though, as anyone who has argued with a teenager about a pierced belly button will attest, people on both sides can come up with a whole slew of arguments). There's some social-psychological truth in the old Flanders & Swann song "The Reluctant Cannibal," about a young "savage" who pushes away from the table and declares, "I won't eat people. Eating people is wrong." His father has all the arguments, such as they are. ("But people have always eaten people, / What else is there to eat? / If the Juju had meant us not to eat people, / He wouldn't have made us of meat!") The son, though, just repeats his newfound conviction: Eating people is wrong. He's just sure of it, he'll say so again and again, and he'll win the day by declamation.

Or take the practice of foot-binding in China, which persisted for a thousand years—and was largely eradicated within a generation. The anti-foot-binding campaign, in the 1910s and 1920s, did circulate facts about the disadvantages of bound feet, but those couldn't have come as news to most people. Perhaps more effective was the campaign's emphasis that no other country went in for the practice; in the world at large, then, China was "losing face" because of it. Natural-foot societies were formed, with members forswearing the practice and further pledging that their sons would not marry women with bound feet. As the movement took hold, scorn was heaped on older women with bound feet, and they were forced to endure the agonies of unbinding. What had been beautiful became ugly; ornamentation became disfigurement. (The success of the anti-foot-binding campaign was undoubtedly a salutary development, but it was not without its victims. Think of some of the last women whose feet were bound, who had to struggle to find husbands.) The appeal to reason alone can explain neither the custom nor its abolition.

So, too, with other social trends. Just a couple of generations ago, in most of the industrialized world, most people thought that middle-class women would ideally be housewives and mothers. If they had time on their hands, they could engage in charitable work or entertain one another; a few of them might engage in the arts, writing novels, painting, performing in music, theater, and dance. But there was little place for them in the "learned professions"— as lawyers or doctors, priests or rabbis; and if they were to be academics, they would teach young women and probably remain unmarried. They were not likely to make their way in politics, except perhaps at the local level. And they were not made welcome in science. How much of the shift away from these assumptions is the result of arguments? Isn't a significant part of it just the consequence of our getting used to new ways of doing things? The arguments that kept the old pattern in place were not—to put it mildly—terribly good. If the *reasons* for the old sexist way of doing things had been the problem, the women's movement could have been done with in a couple of weeks. There are still people,

I know, who think that the ideal life for any woman is making and managing a home. There are more who think that it is an honorable option. Still, the vast majority of Westerners would be appalled at the idea of trying to force women back into these roles. Arguments mattered for the women who made the women's movement and the men who responded to them. This I do not mean to deny. But their greatest achievement has been to change our habits. In the 1950s, if a college-educated woman wanted to go to law or business school, the natural response was "Why?" Now the natural response is "Why not?"

Or consider another example: in much of Europe and North America, in places where a generation ago homosexuals were social outcasts and homosexual acts were illegal, lesbian and gay couples are increasingly being recognized by their families, by society, and by the law. This is true despite the continued opposition of major religious groups and a significant and persisting undercurrent of social disapproval. Both sides make arguments, some good, most bad, if you apply a philosophical standard of reasoning. But if you ask the social scientists what has produced this change, they will rightly not start with a story about reasons. They will give you a historical account that concludes with a sort of perspectival shift. The increasing presence of "openly gay" people in social life and in the media has changed our habits. Over the last thirty or so years, instead of thinking about the private activity of gay *sex*, many Americans started thinking about the public category of gay *people*. Even those who continue to think of the sex with disgust now find it harder to deny these people their respect and concern (and some of them have learned, as we all did with our own parents, that it's better not to think too much about other people's sex lives anyway).

Now, I don't deny that all the time, at every stage, people were talking, giving each other reasons to do things: accept their children, stop treating homosexuality as a medical disorder, disagree with their churches, come out. Still, the short version of the story is basically this: people got used to lesbians and gay people. I am urging that we should learn about people in other places, take an interest in their civilizations, their arguments, their errors, their achievements, not because that will bring us to agreement, but because it will help us get used to one another. If that is the aim, then the fact that we have all these opportunities for disagreement about values need not put us off. Understanding one another may be hard; it can certainly be interesting. But it doesn't require that we come to agreement.

Fighting for the Good

I've said we can live in harmony without agreeing on underlying values (except, perhaps, the cosmopolitan value of living together). It works the other way, too: we can find ourselves in conflict when we do agree on values. Warring parties are seldom at odds because they have clashing conceptions of "the good." On the contrary, conflict arises most often when two peoples have identified the same thing as good. The fact that both Palestinians and Israelis—in particular, that both observant Muslims and observant Jews—have a special relation to Jerusalem, to the Temple Mount, has been a reliable source of trouble. The problem isn't that they disagree about the importance of Jerusalem: the problem is exactly that they both care for it deeply and, in part, for the same reasons. Muhammad, in the first years of Islam, urged his followers to turn toward Jerusalem in prayer because he had learned the story of Jerusalem from the Jews among whom he lived in Mecca. Nor (as we shall see in chapter 9) is it an accident that the West's fiercest adversaries among other societies tend to come from among the most Westernized of the group. *Mon semblable mon frère?* Only if the *frère* you have in mind is Cain. We all know now that the foot soldiers of Al Qaeda who committed the mass murders at the Twin Towers and the Pentagon were not Bedouins from the desert; not unlettered fellahin.

Indeed, there's a wider pattern here. Who in Ghana excoriated the British and built the movement for independence? Not the farmers and the peasants. Not the chiefs. It was the Western-educated bourgeoisie. And when in the 1950s Kwame Nkrumah—who went to college in Pennsylvania and lived in London—created a nationalist mass movement, at its core were soldiers who had returned from fighting a war in the British army, urban market women who traded Dutch prints, trade unionists who worked in industries created by colonialism, and the so-called veranda boys, who had been to colonial secondary schools, learned English, studied history and geography in textbooks written in England. Who led the resistance to the British Raj? An Indian-born South African lawyer, trained in the British courts, whose name was Gandhi; an Indian named Nehru who wore Savile Row suits and sent his daughter to an English boarding school; and Muhammad Ali Jinnah, founder of Pakistan, who joined Lincoln's Inn in London and became a barrister at the age of nineteen.

In Shakespeare's *Tempest,* Caliban, the original inhabitant of an island commandeered by Prospero, roars at his domineering colonizer, "You taught me language and my profit on't / Is, I know how to curse." It is no surprise that Prospero's "abhorred slave" has been a figure of colonial resistance for literary nationalists all around the world. And in borrowing from Caliban, they have also borrowed from Shakespeare. Prospero has told Caliban,

> When thou didst not, savage,
> Know thine own meaning, but wouldst gabble like

A thing most brutish, I endowed thy purposes
With words that made them known.

Of course, one of the effects of colonialism was not only to give many of the natives a European language, but also to help shape their purposes. The independence movements of the post-1945 world that led to the end of Europe's African and Asian empires were driven by the rhetoric that had guided the Allies' own struggle against Germany and Japan: democracy, freedom, equality. This wasn't a conflict between values. It was a conflict of interests couched in terms of the same values.

The point applies as much within the West as elsewhere. Americans disagree about abortion, many vehemently. They couch this conflict in a language of conflicting values: they are pro-life or pro-choice. But this is a dispute that makes sense only because each side recognizes the very values the other insists upon. The disagreement is about their significance. Both sides respect something like the sanctity of human life. They disagree about such things as why human life is so precious and where it begins. Whatever you want to call those disagreements, it's just a mistake to think that either side doesn't recognize the value at stake here. And the same is true about choice: Americans are not divided about whether it's important to allow people, women and men, to make the major medical choices about their own bodies. They are divided about such questions as whether an abortion involves two people—both fetus and mother—or three people, adding in the father, or only one. Furthermore, no sane person on either side thinks that saving human lives or allowing people medical autonomy is the only thing that matters.

Some people will point to disputes about homosexuality and say that there, at least, there really is a conflict between people who do and people who don't regard homosexuality as a perversion. Isn't that a conflict of values? Well, no. Most Americans, on both sides, have the concept of perversion: of sexual acts that are wrong because their objects are inappropriate objects of sexual desire. But not everyone thinks that the fact that an act involves two women or two men makes it perverted. Not everyone who thinks these acts are perverse thinks they should be illegal. Not everyone who thinks they should be illegal thinks that gay and lesbian people should be ostracized. What is at stake, once more, is a battle about the meaning of perversion, about its status as a value, and about how to apply it. It is a reflection of the essentially contestable character of perversion as a term of value. When one turns from the issue of criminalization of gay sex—which is, at least for the moment, unconstitutional in the United States—to the question of gay marriage, all sides of the debate take seriously issues of sexual autonomy, the value of the intimate lives of couples, the meaning of family, and, by way of discussions of perversion, the proper uses of sex.

What makes these conflicts so intense is that they are battles over the meaning of the *same* values, not that they oppose one value, held exclusively by one side, with another, held exclusively by their antagonists. It is, in part, because we have shared horizons of meaning, because these are debates between people who share so many other values and so much else in the way of belief and of habit, that they are as sharp and as painful as they are.

Winners and Losers

But the disputes about abortion and gay marriage divide Americans bitterly most of all because they share a society and a government. They are neighbors and fellow citizens. And it is laws governing all of them that are in dispute. What's at stake are their bodies or those of their mothers, their aunts, their sisters, their daughters, their wives, and their friends; those dead fetuses could have been their children or their children's friends.

We should remember this when we think about international human rights treaties. Treaties are law, even when they are weaker than national law. When we seek to embody our concern for strangers in human rights law and when we urge our government to enforce it, we are seeking to change the world of law in every nation on the planet. We have outlawed slavery not just domestically but in international law. And in so doing we have committed ourselves, at a minimum, to the desirability of its eradication everywhere. This is no longer controversial in the capitals of the world. No one defends enslavement. But international treaties define slavery in ways that arguably include debt bondage; and debt bondage is a significant economic institution in parts of South Asia. I hold no brief for debt bondage. Still, we shouldn't be surprised if people whose income and whose style of life depend upon it are angry. Given that we have neighbors—even if only a few—who think that the fact that abortion is permitted in the United States turns the killing of the doctors who perform them into an act of heroism, we should not be surprised that there are strangers—even if only a few—whose anger turns them to violence against us.

I do not fully understand the popularity among Islamist movements in Egypt, Algeria, Iran, and Pakistan of a high-octane anti-Western rhetoric. But I do know one of its roots. It is, to use suitably old-fashioned language, "the woman question." There are Muslims, many of them young men, who feel that forces from outside their society—forces that they might think of as Western or, in a different moment, American—are pressuring them to reshape relations between men and women. Part of that pressure, they feel, comes from our media. Our films and our television programs are crammed with indescribable indecency. Our fashion magazines show women without modesty, women whose presence on many streets in the Muslim world would be a provocation, they think, presenting an almost irresistible temptation to men. Those magazines influence publications in their own countries, pulling them inevitably in the same direction. We permit women to swim almost naked with strange men, which is our business; but it is hard to keep the news of these acts of immodesty from Muslim women and children or to protect Muslim men from the temptations they inevitably create. As the Internet spreads, it will get even harder, and their children, especially their girls, will be tempted to ask for these freedoms too. Worse, they say, we are now trying to force our conception of how women and men should behave upon them. We speak of women's rights. We make treaties enshrining these rights. And then we want their governments to enforce them.[3]

Like many people in every nation, I support those treaties, of course; I believe that women, like men, should have the vote, should be entitled to work outside their homes, should be protected from the physical abuse of men, including their fathers, brothers, and husbands. But I also know that the changes that these freedoms would bring will change the balance of power between men and women in everyday life. How do I know this? Because I have lived most of my adult life in the West as it has gone through the latter phases of just such a transition, and I know that the process is not yet complete.

The recent history of America does show that a society can radically change its attitudes—and more importantly, perhaps, its habits—about these issues over a single generation. But it also suggests that some people will stay with the old attitudes, and the whole process will take time. The relations between men and women are not abstractions: they are part of the intimate texture of our everyday lives. We have strong feelings about them, and we have inherited many received ideas. Above all, we have deep *habits* about gender. A man and a woman go out on a date. Our habit is that, even if the woman offers, the man pays. A man and a woman approach an elevator door. The man steps back. A man and a woman kiss in a move theater. No one takes a second look. Two men walk hand in hand in the high street. People are embarrassed. They hope their children don't see. They don't know how to explain it to them.

Most Americans are against gay marriage, conflicted about abortion, and amazed (and appalled) that a Saudi woman can't get a driver's license. But my guess is that they're not as opposed to gay marriage as they were twenty years ago. Indeed, twenty years ago, most Americans would probably just have thought the whole idea ridiculous. On the other hand, those Americans who are in favor of recognizing gay marriages probably don't have a simple set of reasons why. It just seems right to them, probably, in the way that it just seems wrong to those who disagree. (And probably they're thinking not about couples in the abstract but about Jim and John or Jean and Jane.) The younger they are, the more likely it is that they think that gay marriage is fine. And if they don't, it will often be because they have had religious objections reinforced regularly through life in church, mosque, or temple.

I am a philosopher. I believe in reason. But I have learned in a life of university teaching and research that even the cleverest people are not easily shifted by reason alone—and that can be true even in the most cerebral of realms. One of the great savants of the postwar era, John von Neumann, liked to say, mischievously, that "in mathematics you don't understand things, you just get used to them." In the larger world, outside the academy, people don't always even care whether they *seem* reasonable. Conversation, as I've said, is hardly guaranteed to lead to agreement about what to think and feel. Yet we go wrong if we think the point of conversation is to persuade, and imagine it proceeding as a debate, in which points are scored for the Proposition and the Opposition. Often enough, as Faust said, in the beginning is the deed: practices and not principles are what enable us to live together in peace. Conversations across boundaries of identity—whether national, religious, or something else—begin with the sort of imaginative engagement you get when you read a novel or watch a movie or attend to a work of art that speaks from some place other than your own. So I'm using the word "conversation" not only for literal talk but also as a metaphor for engagement with the experience and the ideas of others. And I stress the role of the imagination here because the encounters, properly conducted, are valuable in themselves. Conversation doesn't have to lead to consensus about anything, especially not values; it's enough that it helps people get used to one another.

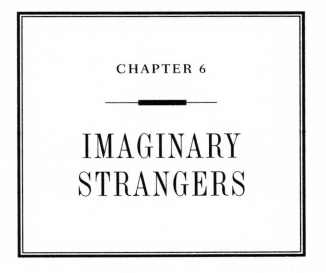

CHAPTER 6

IMAGINARY STRANGERS

Waiting for the King

My mother and I are seated on a large veranda. From its high ceiling, eight fans are turning at full speed, and a light breeze from the garden blows through the screened openings; and so, though it is hot outside, we do not feel hot. Before us, on a dais, is an empty throne, its arms and legs embossed with polished brass, the back and seat covered in a fabric vaguely reminiscent of a scarf by Hermès. In front of the steps to the dais, there are two columns of people, mostly men, facing each other, seated on stools, the cloths they wear wrapped around their chests so that their shoulders are bare. Between them there is an open path to the throne. Around the throne itself are other men; some of them have one shoulder covered, toga-style, so we know they are higher in rank. But in front of them on the top step sits a young man, shoulders bare, holding an umbrella open above the throne.

There is a quiet buzz of conversation. Outside in the garden, peacocks screech. We are waiting for the Asantehene, king of Asante. It is a Wednesday festival day, in Kumasi, during which the king will sit here for a few hours and people will come up to shake his hand, say a few words, pay their respects.

At last, the horn player blows the ram's horn, and its tune tells us that the man we have been waiting for has come, the *kɔtɔkɔhene*—the porcupine chief, the horn names him, for the porcupine has a multitude of quills, each signifying a warrior ready to kill and to die for the kingdom. Everyone stands until he has settled on the throne. Then, when we sit, a chorus of men in the rear sings songs in praise of him, interspersed with the playing of a flute. When, in the course of this music making, I catch his eye, he smiles at me. But mostly he sits there impassively; he has been king for five years now, but he looks as though he could have been sitting in state all his life.

By custom on this day, his first greetings will be for members of the royal family, children and grandchildren of his predecessors on the throne. They will not shake his hand. They will come and bow or curtsey, the men uncovering both shoulders, as one does for all the chiefs of Asante. The rest of us will wait our turn. And when it comes, each of us will be presented by the king's linguist and then summoned up for a word or two of conversation.

When my moment comes, I am introduced by the linguist as my father's son, as a professor at Princeton, as the bearer of some bottles of Dutch schnapps (for several centuries now an appropriate gift for a West African royal) and a gift of money (a million cedis, actually, or about a hundred dollars).

When I step up for my few words, the king asks me how things are in America.

"Fine," I say. "When will you next be in the States?"

"I have to come soon," he tells me. "I'm coming to see Jim Wolfensohn."

So the king of Asante, a kingdom formally part of the modern republic of Ghana, would soon be visiting the then president of the World Bank.

This is, for all but a few million Ghanaians, a relatively unfamiliar world. For visiting English cousins and American friends, it has usually seemed, at first, wonderfully exotic; our tourist industry no doubt depends on this response. Most people elsewhere would think of this Wednesday festival as belonging quaintly to an African past, and this sense would be confirmed by the discovery that today began for the king with a visit to pay his respects to the blackened stools of his ancestors. But as we waited for him, there were people taking calls on cell phones under those whirling fans; and the people who followed me up to greet him were a dozen men in suits, representatives of an insurance company. When the chiefs who pass by greet me, they ask about Princeton. And the meetings in the office next to the veranda are about twenty-first-century issues: the educational needs of twenty-first-century children, HIV/AIDS, the local university of science and technology.

Anywhere you travel in the world—today as always—you can find ceremonies such as these, many of them, like these, rooted in centuries-old traditions. But you will also find everywhere—and this is something new—many intimate connections with places far away: Washington, Moscow, Mexico City, Beijing. Across the street from us, when we were growing up, was a large house occupied by a number of families, among them a vast family of boys; one, about my age, was a good friend. He lives in London now. His brother, who helped look after my father when he was dying, lives in Japan, where his wife is from. They have another brother who has been in Spain for a while and a couple more who, last I heard, were in the United States. Some of them still live in Kumasi, one or two in Accra. Eddie, who lives in Japan, speaks his wife's language now. He has to. But he was never very comfortable in English, the language of our government and our schools. When he phones me from time to time, he prefers to speak Asante-Twi.

Over the years, the palace buildings have expanded. When I was a small child, we used to visit the previous king, my great-uncle by marriage, in a small building that the British had allowed his predecessor to build when he returned from exile in the Seychelles to a restored but diminished Asante kingship. That building is now a museum, dwarfed by the enormous house next door—built by his successor, my uncle by marriage—where the current king lives. Next to it is the suite of offices abutting the veranda where we were sitting, recently finished by the present king, my uncle's successor. The British, my mother's people, con-quered Asante at the turn of the twentieth century; now, at the turn of the twenty-first, the palace feels as it must have felt in the nineteenth century: a center of power. The president of Ghana comes from this world too. He was born across the street from the palace to a member of the royal Oyoko clan. But he belongs to other worlds as well: he went to Oxford University; he's a mem-ber of one of the Inns of Court in London; he's a Catholic, with a picture of himself greeting the pope in his sitting room.

Going Home

Kumasi is where I grew up; but I haven't lived in Ghana for more than thirty years. Like many people today—like, for example, more than a hundred thousand Ghanaians in England—I live a long way away from the home of my earliest memories. Like many, I return there from time to time, to visit family and friends. And, again like many, when I am there I feel both that I do and that I don't belong. At moments like the one at the palace, I know what is happening, and people know who I am. So, in one sense, I fit in. Nothing surprises me. I know how to behave.

On the other hand, there are things in Kumasi that remind me constantly that this is no longer where I live. I find I am irritated, for example, by the slow pace of things, by the unreliability of services. If, as often happens, my mother's phone stops working, it won't just get put right. Someone must go down to the central post office, and then she must wait—days, a week or two, who knows?— until they get around to fixing it. Everyone you talk to will be polite, but they will move to the very slow beat of a drummer of their own. I feel, in short, the way the city mouse feels visiting his country cousins. But, in fact, it's my home in New Jersey that is in the country. There I live outside a small town (population 2,696 in the 2000 census). Kumasi, on the other hand, is the second city of Ghana, with more than half a million people. At its center is the Kejetia market, covering nearly thirty acres; with thousands of traders selling a miscellaneous alphabet of goods from avocados, bicycles, and carburetors to yams and zucchini, it's often said to be the largest market in West Africa.

There's something else about Kumasi, something that probably strikes every tourist eventually: people are constantly asking you for things. It's not just the beggars, of whom there are many, often physically disabled—blind old women and men, accompanied by sighted children who guide them to your car window, polio victims on crutches, lepers with fingers eaten away by disease. Ordinary respectable people will ask, "What did you bring me?" Or, "Can you take me with you to America?" Or, "When you go home will you send me a watch?" (Or a cell phone or a laptop.) They ask you for help with visas and plane tickets and jobs. It may seem as if they have a wildly exaggerated sense of the power and wealth to which you have access simply by living in the industrialized world.

To understand these constant demands you have to understand something about life in Ghana. It is true now, as it was true one and two and three centuries ago, that success in life depends on being enmeshed in a web of relationships. To get things done—to get a driver's license, a passport, a building permit, a job—you need to be someone or know someone with the social standing to work your will. Since most people don't have that status, they need to find someone—a patron—who does. In a society like this, to ask someone for something is to invite him to become your patron. It's a sign that you think he has the status to get things done. And so it's a way of indicating respect. Which explains an old Ashanti proverb that would otherwise seem completely mysterious:

> Obi tan wo a, ɔnsrɛ wo adeɛ.
> *If someone hates you, he won't ask you for things.*

The Romans had a word for these dependents: it was *clientes*. Our word "client" has entirely lost this sense of the mutual dependency of patron and client. The client is now—except in the snootiest of restaurants and boutiques—the boss. In the Roman world, by contrast, as in Asante for the last few centuries, the patron was the boss, and the clients needed him to get on in the world. The patron's status also depended on his being seen to serve his clients: master and man each depend on one another. This is a thought that philosophers often ascribe to Hegel, who has a famous analysis in *The Phenomenology of Spirit* of the dependence of the master on the servitor's regard. But any Roman could have taught you this lesson. The third book of Horace's odes begins with a poem, *Odi profanum vulgus*, that is, in part, about the burdens of wealth and status, the burdens of being a patron. He talks about the security of being someone who "desires only what is enough," and thus is not open to the risks of loss that face the rich. And at one point early in the poem, he talks, too, about a group of candidates for election, entering the public square in Rome. One is from a more noble lineage, one is a stylish fellow with a good reputation, and about the third he says,

> . . . the crowd of that one's clients
> may be greater.

Illi turba clientium sit maior: he may have a larger crowd of clients. Having a host of dependents was a source of status in Augustan Rome. It was something that got you respect; it might even have gotten you elected to office.

If you are not from Kumasi that world may seem, as I say, strange . . . striking and colorful, too, perhaps, but certainly alien. Many of the things that worry people there, many of the projects that engage them, won't be worries and projects of yours. But that doesn't distinguish people in Kumasi from many of your neighbors down the street. You've either been born again or you haven't; whichever side of this divide you're on, you have a very different take on the world from those on the other side. And there's the same division between Pentecostalists and the older mainline denominations of Christianity in Kumasi. More importantly, even if this world strikes you as strange, you can nevertheless make sense of it. You don't know how to behave in Kumasi, but you could learn, as my mother did when she moved here from England half a century ago. Of course, as my Asante kinsmen say, *Ɔmamfrani nnyini kronkron*, "the stranger never grows to perfection." If, like my mother, you move to a place and learn its language in your thirties, you can't expect to get everything right.

And you can *imagine* having beliefs that you don't, in fact, share. No doubt, you don't believe that it's important to keep the royal ancestors happy by placing food offerings on their blackened stools;

but if you believed that their spirits could shape life now, for better or worse, you would want the Asantehene to make his offerings, too. You might find the constant demands of friends and acquaintances mildly disconcerting; but, once the underlying principles of the relationship between patrons and clients has been explained to you, you can understand why they do it.

Finally, there's just a great deal of everyday life that is utterly, humanly familiar. People in Ghana, people everywhere, buy and sell, eat, read the papers, watch movies, sleep, go to church or mosque, laugh, marry, make love, commit adultery, go to funerals, die. Most of the time, once someone has translated the language you don't know, or explained some little unfamiliar symbol or custom, you'll have no more (and, of course, no less) trouble understanding why they do what they do than you do making sense of your neighbors back home.

Do We Need Universals?

Why is it so easy for a human visitor from anywhere to make sense of Asante? One answer, which you will get from cultural psychologists, is that the machinery of the mind is the same everywhere. There must be some sense in which this is true. You need to be careful, though, in parsing the claim. People everywhere see red and green and yellow and blue. Still there are also people born congenitally blind everywhere; and there are tetrachromats, who see more colors than the rest of us, and people with various kinds of color blindness, who see fewer. In what sense, then, is it true that human color vision is universal? The world's finest musicians and mathematicians come from all over the planet: but there is something about the machinery of their minds that we do not all share. In Euclid there's a theorem known as the *pons asinorum,* the bridge of asses. Mathematical incompetents, it was said—the asses—couldn't get across. You could give Suzuki classes to everyone; only a few will end up playing like Yo-Yo Ma. In what sense are the cognitive capacities for mathematics and music universal? You will find people everywhere who are kindly, sympathizing with others. But there are sociopaths and psychopaths scattered across the planet, too. In what sense are kindness and sympathy universal? The answer in each case is not that *every* human being has these traits or capacities. Rather, they are present in every large enough group of our species; in particular, they are the statistical norm in every society.

Now, it is quite contingent that these particular skills and capacities are distributed in this way. It could have been that there was a valley where everyone was red-green color-blind. Anthropologists and psychologists and linguists would troop to the place, and, as H. G. Wells implied in *The Country of the Blind,* it might well turn out that it would be the visitors who would be at a disadvantage. (Plenty of our fellow mammals do quite well without color vision.) Still, it's presumably just because there isn't such a place that there's a pattern to the way basic color terms work in every human language. As Brent Berlin and Paul Kay showed, in their book *Basic Color Terms: Their Universality and Evolution,* there is a (rather complex) cross-cultural pattern to the way basic color terms work. A basic color term is, roughly, a term—like "blue," but unlike "sky blue"—whose meaning isn't composed from meaningful parts. Languages vary in the number of basic color terms they have; but Berlin and Kay argued that the evidence showed that they always have black and white, and that if they add further basic color terms, they add them in the same sequence, starting with red, followed by yellow or green, up to a total of eleven basic colors.[1] Later studies have not confirmed all the details of their account. But the broad outline of their story is now widely accepted.

Color language is a good example of the way in which basic features of most normal people—the way our retinas and visual cortexes work, and the inbuilt capacity for learning a language—are shaped by experience and by culture. Someone who was raised inside a house where everything was painted black or white, wore only those colors, was surrounded by people dressed likewise, and was exposed only to black and white food, and so forth could understand only those color terms (and, of course, the names for colors found on the human body). Whether you have a word for the color purple, on the other hand, won't just depend on whether you've ever seen something purple; it will depend, too, on the resources of your language.

Cross-cultural analysis reveals that there really are some basic mental traits that are universal—in the sense that they're normal everywhere. It has also confirmed, for that matter, that some unusual traits—the incapacity to make sense of other people that we call autism—are found in every human population, too. Building on these traits, on our biological natures, cultures produce a great deal of variety, but also much that is the same. Part of the reason for this is that, in culture as in biology, our human environment presents similar problems; and societies, like natural selection, often settle on the same solution because it is the best available. Donald Brown, in his book *Human Universals,* has a fascinating chapter called "The Universal People," which describes many of the traits we humans share. As with all scholarship, it contains claims that other serious scholars would deny. It is hard, though, to resist the evidence that, starting with our common biology and the shared problems of the human situation (and granted that we may also share cultural traits because of our common origins), human societies have ended up having many deep things in common.[2] Among them are practices like music, poetry, dance, marriage, funerals; values resembling courtesy, hospitality, sexual modesty, generosity, reciprocity, the resolution of social conflict; concepts such as good and evil, right and wrong, parent and child, past, present, and future. "If a lion could speak," Ludwig Wittgenstein wrote, "we couldn't understand him." It's a shared human nature, he meant, that allows us to make sense of one another.

But my ability to connect with people in a Chinese village, or your ability to figure out what is going on in Kumasi or Kuala Lumpur or Kalamazoo, doesn't depend just on what all human beings share. When two normal people meet, they often share not only what all normal human beings share but also much else. This is one result of the constant contact across societies produced by our traveling habits and the trade in goods, both physical and symbolic, that now connects us all. The cosmopolitan curiosity about other peoples does not have to begin by seeking in each encounter those traits that all humans share. In some encounters, what we start with is some small thing we two singular people share. Around the world there are people who are fascinated by astrology or insects or the history of warfare or Zeno's paradox. Interest in none of these things is a human universal. (I have failed to get people interested in Zeno's paradox in three continents.) Nevertheless, interests like these can and do connect people across societies.

The conclusion is obvious enough: the points of entry to cross-cultural conversations are things that are shared by those who are in the conversation. They do not need to be universal; all they need to be is what these particular people have in common. Once we have found enough we share, there is the further possibility that we will be able to enjoy discovering things we do not yet share. That is one of the payoffs of cosmopolitan curiosity. We can learn from one another; or we can simply be intrigued by alternative ways of thinking, feeling, and acting.

There is a clue here to what I think is a deep and important rejoinder to a common form of skepticism about the cosmopolitan enterprise. "You are asking us," the skeptic says, "to care about all human beings. But we care only about people with whom we share an identity—national, familial, religious, or the like. And those identities get their psychological energy from the fact that to every in-group there's an out-group. Loving America has, in part, to be about hating, or anyway disliking, America's enemies: amity is the daughter of strife. And the trouble with humanity, as an identity, is that, until the *War of the Worlds* begins, there is no out-group to generate the binding energy that every in-group needs." (Sometimes humanists want to respond that our fellow animals provide an out-group. This seems to me false to human psychology. Out-groups have to be people: creatures with languages, projects, cultures.) The force of the objection is not that we can't take a moral interest in strangers, but that the interest is bound to be abstract, lacking in the warmth and power that comes from shared identity. Humanity isn't, in the relevant sense, an identity at all.

Suppose, for the moment, that all this is right. (Though, as you'll see at the end of chapter 8, I think this objection gets something seriously wrong.) Still, engagement with strangers is always going to be engagement with particular strangers; and the warmth that comes from shared identity will often be available. Some American Christians send money to suffering fellow Christians in southern Sudan; writers, through PEN International, campaign for the freedom of other writers, imprisoned around the world; women in Sweden work for women's rights in South Asia; Indians in the Punjab worry about the fate of Punjabis in Canada and Britain. I care about some people in other places, people whose oppression would engage me particularly, just because I have read their philosophical writings, admired their novels, seen them play spectacular games of tennis on television. So, if we change the examples to suit the case, do you.

The problem of cross-cultural communication can seem

immensely difficult in theory, when we are trying to imagine making sense of a stranger in the abstract. But the great lesson of anthropology is that when the stranger is no longer imaginary, but real and present, sharing a human social life, you may like or dislike him, you may agree or disagree; but, if it is what you both want, you can make sense of each other in the end.

CHAPTER 7

COSMOPOLITAN CONTAMINATION

Global Villages

People who complain about the homogeneity produced by globalization often fail to notice that globalization is, equally, a threat to homogeneity. You can see this as clearly in Kumasi as anywhere. The capital of Asante is accessible to you, whoever you are—emotionally, intellectually, and, of course, physically. It is integrated into the global markets. None of this makes it Western, or American, or British. It is still Kumasi. What it isn't, just because it's a city, is homogeneous. English, German, Chinese, Syrian, Lebanese, Burkinabe, Ivorian, Nigerian, Indian: I can find you families of each description. I can find you Asante people, whose ancestors have lived in this town for centuries, but also Hausa households that have been around for centuries, too. There are people there from all the regions, speaking all the scores of languages of Ghana as well. And while people in Kumasi come from a wider variety of places than they did a hundred or two hundred years ago, even then there were already people from all over the place coming and going. I don't know who was the first Asante to make the pilgrimage to Mecca, but his trip would have followed trade routes that are far older than the kingdom. Gold, salt, kola nuts, and, alas, slaves have connected my hometown to the world for a very long time. And trade means travelers. If by globalization you have in mind something new and recent, the ethnic eclecticism of Kumasi is not the result of it.

But if you go outside Kumasi, only a little way—twenty miles, say, in the right direction—and if you drive off the main road down one of the many potholed side roads of red laterite, you can arrive pretty soon in villages that are fairly homogeneous. The people have mostly been to Kumasi and seen the big, polyglot, diverse world of the city. Here, though, where they live, there is one everyday language (aside from the English in the government schools), a few Asante families, and an agrarian way of life that is based on some old crops, like yam, and some new ones, like cocoa, which arrived in the late nineteenth century as a commercial product for export. They may or may not have electricity (this close to Kumasi, they probably do). When people talk of the homogeneity produced by globalization, what they are talking about is this: the villagers will have radios; you will be able to get a discussion going about the World Cup in soccer, Muhammad Ali, Mike Tyson, and hip-hop; and you will probably be able to find a bottle of Guinness or Coca-Cola (as well as Star or Club, Ghana's own delicious lagers). Then again, the language on the radio won't be a world language, the soccer teams they know best will be Ghanaian, and what can you tell about someone's soul from the fact that she drinks Coca-Cola? These villages are connected with more places than they were a couple of centuries ago. Their homogeneity, though, is still the local kind.

In the era of globalization—in Asante as in New Jersey—people make pockets of homogeneity. Are all these pockets of homogeneity less distinctive than they were a century ago? Well, yes, but mostly in good ways. More of them have access to medicines that work. More of them have access to clean drinking water. More of them have schools. Where, as is still too common, they don't have these things, this is not something to celebrate but to deplore. And whatever loss of difference there has been, they are constantly inventing new forms of difference: new hairstyles, new slang, even, from time to time, new religions. No one could say that the world's villages are—or are about to become—anything like the same.

So why do people in these places sometimes feel that their identity is threatened? Because the world, their world, is changing, and some of them don't like it. The pull of the global economy—witness those cocoa trees whose chocolate is eaten all around the world—created some of the life they now live. If the economy changes—if cocoa prices collapse again as they did in the early 1990s—they may have to find new crops or new forms of livelihood. That is unsettling for some people (just as it is exciting for others). Missionaries came a while ago, so many of these villagers will be Christian, even if they also have kept some of the rites from earlier days. But new Pentecostal messengers are challenging the churches they know and condemning the old rites as idolatrous. Again, some like it; some don't.

Above all, relationships are changing. When my father was young, a man in a village would farm some land that a chief had granted him, and his *abusua,* his matriclan, (including his younger brothers) would work it with him. If extra hands were needed in the harvest season, he would pay the migrant workers who came from the north. When a new house needed building, he would organize it. He would also make sure his dependents were fed and clothed, the children educated, marriages and funerals arranged and paid for. He could expect to pass the farm and the responsibilities eventually to one of his nephews.

Nowadays, everything has changed. Cocoa prices have not kept pace with the cost of living. Gas prices have made the transportation of the crop more expensive. And there are new possibilities for the young in the towns, in other parts of the country, and in other parts of the world. Once, perhaps, you could have commanded your nephews and nieces to stay. Now they have the right to leave; in any case, you may not make enough to feed and clothe and educate them all. So the time of the successful farming family has gone; and those who were settled in that way of life are as sad to see it go as some of the American family farmers whose lands are being accumulated by giant agribusinesses. We can sympathize with them. But we cannot force their children to stay in the name of protecting their authentic culture; and we cannot afford to subsidize indefinitely thousands of distinct islands of homogeneity that no longer make economic sense.

Nor should we want to. Cosmopolitans think human variety matters because people are entitled to the options they need to shape their lives in partnership with others. What John Stuart Mill said more than a century ago in *On Liberty* about diversity within a society serves just as well as an argument for variety across the globe:

> If it were only that people have diversities of taste, that is reason enough for not attempting to shape them all after one model. But different persons also require different conditions for their spiritual development; and can no more exist healthily in the same moral, than all the variety of plants can exist in the same physical, atmosphere and climate. The same things which are helps to one person towards the cultivation of his higher nature, are hindrances to another. . . . Unless there is a corresponding diversity in their

modes of life, they neither obtain their fair share of happiness, nor grow up to the mental, moral, and aesthetic stature of which their nature is capable.[1]

If we want to preserve a wide range of human conditions because it allows free people the best chance to make their own lives, there is no place for the enforcement of diversity by trapping people within a kind of difference they long to escape. There simply is no decent way to sustain those communities of difference that will not survive without the free allegiance of their members.

Don't Ever Change

Even if you grant that people shouldn't be forced into sustaining authentic cultural practices, you might suppose that a cosmopolitan should side with those who are busy around the world "preserving culture" and resisting "cultural imperialism." But behind these slogans you often find some curious assumptions. Take "preserving culture." It's one thing to provide people with help to sustain arts they want to sustain. I am all for festivals of Welsh bards in Llandudno funded by the Welsh Arts Council, if there are people who want to recite and people who care to listen. I am delighted with the Ghana National Cultural Center in Kumasi, where you can go and learn traditional Akan dancing and drumming, especially since its classes are spirited and overflowing. Restore the deteriorating film stock of early Hollywood movies; continue the preservation of Old Norse and early Chinese and Ethiopian manuscripts; record, transcribe, and analyze the oral narratives of Malay and Maasai and Maori: all these are a valuable part of our human heritage. But preserving *culture*—in the sense of cultural artifacts, broadly conceived—is different from preserving *cultures*. And the preservers of cultures are busy trying to ensure that the Huli of Papua New Guinea or, for that matter, Sikhs in Toronto or Hmong in New Orleans keep their "authentic" ways. What makes a cultural expression authentic, though? Are we to stop the importation of baseball caps into Vietnam, so that the Zao will continue with their colorful red headdresses? Why not ask the Zao? Shouldn't the choice be theirs?

"They *have* no real choice," the cultural preservationists may say. "We have dumped cheap Western clothes into their markets; and they can no longer afford the silk they used to wear. If they had what they really wanted, they'd still be dressed traditionally." Notice that this is no longer an argument about authenticity. The claim is that they can't afford to do something that they'd really like to do, something that is expressive of an identity they care about and want to sustain. This is a genuine problem, one that afflicts people in many communities: they're too poor to live the life they want to lead. If that's true, it's an argument for trying to see whether we can help them get richer. But if they do get richer and they still run around in T-shirts, so much the worse, I say, for authenticity.

Not that this is likely to be a problem in the real world. People who can afford it mostly *like* to put on traditional garb from time to time. American boys wear tuxedos to proms. I was best man once at a Scottish wedding. The bridegroom wore a kilt, of course. (I wore a *kɛntɛ* cloth. Andrew Oransay, who piped us up the aisle, whispered in my ear at one point, "Here we all are then, in our tribal gear.") In Kumasi, people who can afford them, love to put on their *kɛntɛ* cloths, especially the most "traditional" ones, woven in colorful silk strips in the town of Bonwire, as they have been for a couple of centuries. (The prices have risen in part because demand outside Asante has risen. A fine *kɛntɛ* for a man now costs more than the average Ghanaian earns in a year. Is that bad? Not for the people of Bonwire.) But trying to find some primordially authentic culture can be like peeling an onion. The textiles most people think of as traditional West African cloths are known as java prints, and arrived with the Javanese batiks sold, and often milled by, the Dutch. The traditional garb of Herero women derives from the attire of nineteenth-century German missionaries, though it's still unmistakably Herero, not least because the fabrics they use have a distinctly un-Lutheran range of colors. And so with our *kɛntɛ* cloth: the silk was always imported, traded by Europeans, produced in Asia. This tradition was once an innovation. Should we reject *it* for that reason as untraditional? How far back must one go? Should we condemn the young men and women of the University of Science and Technology, a few miles outside Kumasi, who wear European-style gowns for graduation, lined with *kɛntɛ* strips (as they do, now, at Howard and Morehouse, too). Cultures are made of continuities *and* changes, and the identity of a society can survive through these changes, just as each individual survives the alterations of Jacques's "seven ages of man."

The Trouble with "Cultural Imperalism"

Cultural preservationists often make their case by invoking the evil of "cultural imperialism." And its victims aren't necessarily the formerly colonized "natives." In fact, the French have a penchant for talking of "cultural imperialism" to make the point that French people like to watch American movies and visit English-language sites on the Internet. (*Évidemment*, the American taste for French movies is something to be encouraged.) This is surely very odd. No army, no threat of sanctions, no political saber rattling, imposes Hollywood on the French.

There is a genuine issue here, I think, but it is not imperialism. France's movie industry requires government subsidy. Part of the reason, no doubt, is just that Americans have the advantage of speaking a language with many more speakers than France (though this can't be the whole explanation, since the British film industry seems to require subsidy, too). Still, whatever the reason, the French would like to have a significant number of films rooted deeply in French life, which they watch alongside all those American movies. Since the resulting films are often wonderful, in subsidizing them for themselves, they have also enriched the treasury of cosmopolitan cultural experience. So far, I think, so good.

What would justify genuine concern would be an attempt by the United States through the World Trade Organization, say, to have these culturally motivated subsidies banned. Even in the United States, most of us believe it is perfectly proper to subsidize programs on public television. We grant tax-exempt status to our opera and ballet companies; cities and states subsidize sports stadiums. It is an empirical question, not one to be settled by appeal to a free-market ideology, how much of the public culture the citizens of a democratic nation want can be produced solely by the market.

But to concede this much is not to accept what the theorists of cultural imperialism want. In broad strokes, their underlying picture is this. There is a world system of capitalism. It has a center and a periphery. At the center—in Europe and the United States—is a set of multinational corporations. Some of these are in the media business. The products they sell around the world promote the interests of capitalism in general. They encourage consumption not just of films, television, and magazines but of the other non-media products of multinational capitalism. Herbert Schiller, a leading critic of "media/cultural imperialism" has claimed that it is "the imagery and cultural perspectives of the ruling sector in the center that shape and structure consciousness throughout the system at large."[2]

People who believe this story have been taking the pitches of magazine and television company executives selling advertising space for a description of reality. The evidence doesn't bear it out. As it happens, researchers actually went out into the world and explored the responses to the hit television series *Dallas* in Holland and among Israeli Arabs, Moroccan Jewish immigrants, kibbutzniks, and new Russian immigrants to Israel. They have examined the actual content of the television media—whose penetration of every-day life far exceeds that of film—in Australia, Brazil, Canada, India, and Mexico. They have looked at how American popular culture was taken up by the artists of Sophiatown, in South Africa. They have discussed *Days of Our Lives* and the *The Bold and the Beautiful* with Zulu college students from traditional backgrounds.[3]

And they have found two things, which you might already have guessed. The first is that, if there is a local product—as there is in France, but also in Australia, Brazil, Canada, India, Mexico, and South Africa—many people prefer it, especially when it comes to television. For more than a decade in Ghana, the one program you could discuss with almost anyone was a local soap opera in Twi called *Osofo Dadzie*, a lighthearted program with a serious message, each episode, about the problems of contemporary everyday life. We know, do we not, how the Mexicans love their *telenovelas*? (Indeed, people know it even in Ghana, where they are shown in crudely dubbed English versions, too.) The academic research confirms that people tend to prefer television programming that's close to their own cul-ture.[4] (The Hollywood blockbuster has a special status around the world; but here, as American movie critics regularly complain, the nature of the product—heavy on the action sequences, light on clever badinage—is partly determined by what works in Bangkok and Berlin. From the point of view of the cultural-imperialism the-orists, this is a case in which the empire has struck back.)

The second observation that the research supports is that how people respond to these American products depends on their exist-ing cultural context. When the media scholar Larry Strelitz spoke to those students from KwaZulu-Natal, he found that they were anything but passive vessels. One of them, Sipho, reported both that he was a "very, very strong Zulu man" and that he had drawn les-sons from watching the American soap opera *Days of Our Lives*—"especially relationship-wise." It fortified his view that "if a guy can tell a woman that he loves her she should be able to do the same." What's more, after watching the show, Sipho "realized that I should be allowed to speak to my father. He should be my friend rather than just my father. . . ." One doubts that that was the intended message of multinational capitalism's ruling sector.

But Sipho's response also confirmed what has been discovered over and over again. Cultural consumers are not dupes. They can resist. So he also said,

> In terms of our culture, a girl is expected to enter into relationships when she is about 20. In the Western culture, the girl can be exposed to a relationship as early as 15 or 16. That one we should-n't adopt in our culture. Another thing we shouldn't adopt from the Western culture has to do with the way they treat elderly people. I wouldn't like my family to be sent into an old-age home.[5]

The "old-age homes" in American soap operas may be safe places, full of kindly people. That doesn't sell the idea to Sipho. Dutch viewers of *Dallas* saw not the pleasures of conspicuous consump-tion among the super-rich—the message that theorists of "cul-tural imperialism" find in every episode—but a reminder that money and power don't protect you from tragedy. Israeli Arabs saw a program that confirmed that women abused by their hus-bands should return to their fathers. Mexican *telenovelas* remind Ghanaian women that, where sex is at issue, men are not to be trusted. If the *telenovelas* tried to tell them otherwise, they wouldn't believe it.

Talk of cultural imperialism structuring the consciousnesses of those in the periphery treats Sipho and people like him as tabulae rasae on which global capitalism's moving finger writes its message, leaving behind another homogenized consumer as it moves on. It is deeply condescending. And it isn't true.

In Praise of Contamination

Behind much of the grumbling about the cultural effects of globalization is an image of how the world used to be—an image that is both unrealistic and unappealing. Our guide to what is wrong here might as well be another African. Publius Terentius Afer, whom we know as Terence, was born a slave in Carthage in North Africa, and taken to Rome in the late second century AD. Before long, his plays were widely admired among the city's literary elite; witty, elegant works that are, with Plautus's earlier, less cultivated works, essentially all we have of Roman comedy. Terence's own mode of writing—his free incorporation of earlier Greek plays into a single Latin drama—was known to Roman littérateurs as "contamination." It's a suggestive term. When people speak for an ideal of cultural purity, sustaining the authentic culture of the Asante or the American family farm, I find myself drawn to *contamination* as the name for a counter-ideal. Terence had a notably firm grasp on the range of human variety: "So many men, so many opinions" was an observation of his. And it's in his comedy *The Self-Tormentor* that you'll find what has proved something like the golden rule of cosmopolitanism: *Homo sum: humani nil a me alienum puto.* "I am human: nothing human is alien to me." The context is illuminating. The play's main character, a busybody farmer named Chremes, is told by his overworked neighbor to mind his own affairs; the *homo sum* credo is his breezy rejoinder. It isn't meant to be an ordinance from on high; it's just the case for gossip.

Then again, gossip—the fascination people have for the small doings of *other* people—shares a taproot with literature. Certainly the ideal of contamination has no more eloquent exponent than Salman Rushdie, who has insisted that the novel that occasioned his fatwa "celebrates hybridity, impurity, intermingling, the transformation that comes of new and unexpected combinations of human beings, cultures, ideas, politics, movies, songs. It rejoices in mongrelization and fears the absolutism of the Pure. Mélange, hotchpotch, a bit of this and a bit of that is how newness enters the world. It is the great possibility that mass migration gives the world, and I have tried to embrace it."⁶ But it didn't take modern mass migration to create this great possibility. The early Cynics and Stoics took their contamination from the places they were born to the Greek cities where they taught. Many were strangers in those places; cosmopolitanism was invented by contaminators whose migrations were solitary. And the migrations that have contaminated the larger world were not all modern. Alexander's empire molded both the states and the sculpture of Egypt and North India; first the Mongols then the Mughals shaped great swaths of Asia; the Bantu migrations populated half the African continent. Islamic states stretch from Morocco to Indonesia; Christianity reached Africa, Europe, and Asia within a few centuries of the death of Jesus of Nazareth; Buddhism long ago migrated from India into much of East and Southeast Asia. Jews and people whose ancestors came from many parts of China have long lived in vast diasporas. The traders of the Silk Road changed the style of elite dress in Italy; someone brought Chinese pottery for burial in fifteenth-century Swahili graves. I have heard it said that the bagpipes started out in Egypt and came to Scotland with the Roman infantry. None of this is modern.

No doubt, there can be an easy and spurious utopianism of "mixture," as there is of "purity." And yet the larger human truth is on the side of Terence's contamination. We do not need, have never needed, settled community, a homogeneous system of values, in order to have a home. Cultural purity is an oxymoron. The odds are that, culturally speaking, you already live a cosmopolitan life, enriched by literature, art, and film that come from many places, and that contains influences from many more. And the marks of cosmopolitanism in that Asante village—soccer, Muhammad Ali, hip-hop—entered their lives, as they entered yours, not as work but as pleasure. There are some Western products and vendors that appeal to people in the rest of the world *because* they're seen as Western, as modern: McDonald's, Levis. But even here, cultural significance isn't just something that corporate headquarters gets to decree. People wear Levis on every continent. In some places they are informal wear; in others they're dressy. You can get Coca-Cola on every continent, too. In Kumasi you will get it at funerals. Not, in my experience, in the West of England, where hot milky Indian tea is favored. The point is that people in each place make their own uses even of the most famous global commodities.

A tenable cosmopolitanism tempers a respect for difference with a respect for actual human beings—and with a sentiment best captured in the credo, once comic, now commonplace, penned by that former slave from North Africa. Few remember what Chremes says next, but it's as important as the sentence everyone quotes: "Either I want to find out for myself or I want to advise you: think what you like. If you're right, I'll do what you do. If you're wrong, I'll set you straight."

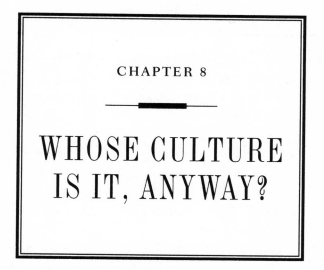

CHAPTER 8

WHOSE CULTURE IS IT, ANYWAY?

The Spoils of War

In the nineteenth century, the kings of Asante—like kings every-where—enhanced their glory by gathering objects from all around their kingdom and around the world. When the British general Sir Garnet Wolseley destroyed Kumasi in a "punitive expedition" in 1874, he authorized the looting of the palace of the Asante king Kofi Karikari. At the treaty of Fomena, a few months later, Asante was required to pay an "indemnity" of 50,000 ounces (nearly one and a half tons) of gold, much of which was delivered in the form of jewelry and other regalia. A couple of decades later, a Major Robert Stephenson Smyth Baden-Powell (yes, you know him as the founder of the Boy Scouts) was dispatched once more to Kumasi, this time to demand that the new king, Prempeh, submit to British rule. Baden-Powell described this mission in his book

The Downfall of Prempeh: A Diary of Life with the Native Levy in Ashanti, 1895–96.

Once the king and his Queen Mother had made their submission, the British troops entered the palace, and, as Baden-Powell put it, "the work of collecting valuables and property was proceeded with." He continued,

> There could be no more interesting, no more tempting work than this. To poke about in a barbarian king's palace, whose wealth has been reported very great, was enough to make it so. Perhaps one of the most striking features about it was that the work of collecting the treasures was entrusted to a company of British soldiers, and that it was done most honestly and well, without a single case of looting. Here was a man with an armful of gold-hilted swords, there one with a box full of gold trinkets and rings, another with a spirit-case full of bottles of brandy, yet in no instance was there any attempt at looting.

This boast will strike us as almost comical, but Baden-Powell clearly believed that the inventorying and removal of these treasures under the orders of a British officer was a legitimate transfer of property. It wasn't looting; it was *collecting*. In short order, Nana Prempeh was arrested and taken into exile at Cape Coast. More indemnities were paid.[1]

There are similar stories to be told around the world. The Belgian *Musée Royal de l'Afrique Centrale*, at Tervuren, explored the dark side of the origins of its own collections in the brutal history of the Belgian Congo, in a 2001 show called "ExItCongoMuseum." The Berlin Museum of Ethnology bought most of its extraordinary Yoruba art from Leo Frobenius, whose methods of "collection" were not exactly limited to free-market exchange.

The modern market in African art, indeed in art from much of the global south, is often a dispiriting sequel to these earlier imperial expropriations. Many of the poorest countries in the world simply do not have the resources to enforce the regulations they make. Mali can declare it illegal to dig up and export the wonderful sculpture of Djenné-Jeno. But it can't enforce the law. And it certainly can't afford to fund thousands of archaeological digs. The result is that many fine Djenné-Jeno terra-cottas were dug up anyway in the 1980s, after the publication of the discoveries of the archaeologists Roderick and Susan McIntosh and their team. They were sold to collectors in Europe and North America who rightly admired them. Because they were removed from archaeological sites illegally, much of what we would most like to know about this culture—much that we could have found out by careful archaeology—may now never be known.

Once the governments of the United States and Mali, guided by archaeologists, created laws specifically aimed at stopping the smuggling of the stolen art, the open market for Djenné-Jeno sculpture largely ceased. But people have estimated that, in the meantime, perhaps a thousand pieces—some of them now valued at hundreds of thousands of dollars—left Mali illegally. Given these enormous prices, you can see why so many Malians were willing to help export their "national heritage."

Modern thefts have not, of course, been limited to the pillaging of archaeological sites. Hundreds of millions of dollars worth of art has been stolen from the museums of Nigeria alone, almost always with the complicity of insiders. And Ekpo Eyo, who once headed the National Museum of Nigeria, has rightly pointed out that dealers in New York and London—dealers including Sotheby's—have been less than eager to assist in their retrieval. Since many of these collections were well known to experts on Nigerian art, it shouldn't have taken the dealers long to recognize what was going on. Nor is such art theft limited to the Third World. Ask the government of Italy.

Given these circumstances—and this history—it has been natural to protest against the pillaging of "cultural patrimony."[2] Through a number of declarations from UNESCO and other international bodies, a doctrine has evolved concerning the ownership of many forms of cultural property. It is that, in simplest terms, cultural property be regarded as the property of its culture. If you belong to that culture, such work is, in the suggestive shorthand, your cultural patrimony. If not, not.

The Patrimony Perplex

Part of what makes this grand phrase so powerful, I suspect, is that it conflates, in confusing ways, the two primary uses of that confusing word "culture." On the one hand, cultural patrimony refers to cultural artifacts: works of art, religious relics, manuscripts, crafts, musical instruments, and the like. Here "culture" is whatever people make and invest with significance through the exercise of their human creativity. Since significance is something produced through conventions, which are never individual and rarely universal, interpreting culture in this sense requires some knowledge of its social and historical context. On the other hand, "cultural patrimony" refers to the products of *a* culture: the group from whose conventions the object derives its significance. Here the objects are understood to belong to a particular group, heirs to a trans-historical identity, whose patrimony they are. The cultural patrimony of Norway, then, is not just Norway's contribution to human culture—its voices in our noisy human chorus, its contribution, as the French might say, to the civilization of the universal. Rather, it is all the artifacts produced by Norwegians, conceived of as a historically persisting people: and while the rest of us may admire Norway's patrimony, it belongs, in the end, to them.

But what does it mean, exactly, for something to belong to a people? Much of Norway's cultural patrimony was produced before the modern Norwegian state existed. (Norway achieved its modern independent existence in 1905, having been conjoined with either Denmark or Sweden—with the exception of a few chaotic months in 1814—since the early fourteenth century.) The Vikings who made the wonderful gold and iron work in the National Museum Building in Oslo didn't think of themselves as the inhabitants of a single country that ran a thousand miles north from the Oslo fjord to the lands of the Sámi reindeer herders. Their identities were tied up, as we learn from the sagas, with lineage and locality. And they would certainly have been astonished to be told that Olaf's gold cup or Thorfinn's sword belonged not to Olaf and Thorfinn and their descendants but to a nation. The Greeks claim the Elgin marbles, which were made not by Greece—it wasn't a state when they were made—but by Athens, when it was a city-state of a few thousand people. When Nigerians claim a Nok sculpture as part of their patrimony, they are claiming for a nation whose boundaries are less than a century old, the works of a civilization more than two millennia ago, created by a people that no longer exists, and whose descendants we know nothing about. We don't know whether Nok sculptures were commissioned by kings or commoners; we don't know whether the people who made them and the people who paid for them thought of them as belonging to the kingdom, to a man, to a lineage, to the gods. One thing we know for sure, however, is that they didn't make them for Nigeria.

Indeed, a great deal of what people wish to protect as "cultural patrimony" was made before the modern system of nations came into being, by members of societies that no longer exist. People die when their bodies die. Cultures, by contrast, can die without physical extinction. So there's no reason to think that the Nok have no descendants. But if Nok civilization came to an end and its people became something else, why should those descendants have a special claim on those objects, buried in the forest and forgotten for so long? And, even if they do have a special claim, what has that got to do with Nigeria, where, let us suppose, a majority of those descendants now live?

Perhaps the matter of biological descent is a distraction: proponents of the patrimony argument would surely be undeterred if it turned out that the Nok sculptures were made by eunuchs. They could reply that the Nok sculptures were found on the territory of Nigeria. And it is, indeed, a perfectly reasonable property rule that where something of value is dug up and nobody can establish an existing claim on it, the government gets to decide what to do with it. It's an equally sensible idea that the object's being of cultural value places on the government a special obligation to preserve it. Given that it is the Nigerian government, it will naturally focus on preserving it for Nigerians (most of whom, not thinking of themselves as heirs to Nok civilization, will probably think it about as interesting as art from anywhere else). But if it is of cultural value—as the Nok sculptures undoubtedly are—it strikes me that it would be better for them to think of themselves as trustees for humanity. While the government of Nigeria reasonably exercises trusteeship, the Nok sculptures belong in the deepest sense to all of us. "Belong" here is a metaphor, of course: I just mean that the Nok sculptures are of potential value to all human beings.

That idea is expressed in the preamble of the Convention for the Protection of Cultural Property in the Event of Armed Conflict of May 14, 1954, which came out of a conference called by UNESCO.

Being convinced that damage to cultural property belonging to
any people whatsoever means damage to the cultural heritage of
all mankind, since each people makes its contribution to the culture of the world. . . .

Framing the problem that way—as an issue for *all* mankind—
should make it plain that it is the value of the cultural property to people and not to peoples that matters. It isn't peoples who experience
and value art; it's men and women. Once you see that, then there's
no reason why a Spanish museum couldn't or shouldn't preserve a
Norse goblet, legally acquired, let us suppose at a Dublin auction,
after the salvage of a Viking shipwreck off Ireland. It's a contribution to the cultural heritage of the world. But at any particular time
it has to be in one place. Don't Spaniards have a case for being able
to experience Viking craftsmanship? After all, there's already an awful
lot of Viking stuff in Norway. The logic of "cultural patrimony" would
call for it to be shipped back to Norway (or, at any rate, to
Scandinavia): that's whose cultural patrimony it is.

And, in various ways, we've inched closer to that position in
the years since the Hague convention. The Convention on the
Means of Prohibiting and Preventing the Illicit Import, Export and
Transfer of Ownership of Cultural Property, adopted by the
UNESCO General Conference in Paris in 1970, stipulated that
"cultural property constitutes one of the basic elements of civilization and national culture, and that its true value can be appreciated
only in relation to the fullest possible information regarding its ori-
gin, history and traditional setting"; that "it is essential for every
State to become increasingly alive to the moral obligations to respect
its own cultural heritage." And a state's cultural heritage, it further
decreed, included both work "created by the individual or collective genius of nationals of the State" and "cultural property found

within the national territory." The convention emphasized, accordingly, the importance of "prohibiting and preventing the illicit import, export and transfer of ownership of cultural property." A number of countries now declare all antiquities that originate within their borders to be state property, which cannot be freely exported. In Italy, private citizens are free to own "cultural property," but not to send it abroad.[3]

Precious Bane

Plainly, special problems are posed by objects, like Viking treasure and Nok art, where there is, as the lawyers might say, no continuity of title. If we don't know who last owned a thing, we need a rule as to what should happen to it now. Where objects have this special status as a valuable "contribution to the culture of the world," the rule should be one that protects that object and makes it available to people who will benefit from experiencing it. So the rule of "finders, keepers," which may make sense for objects of less significance, will not do. Still, a sensible regime will reward those who find such objects, and give them an incentive to report not only what they have found but where and how they found it.

For an object from an archaeological site, after all, value comes often as much from the knowledge to be gleaned by knowing where it came out of the ground, what else was around it, how it lay in the earth. Since these articles usually don't have current owners, someone needs to regulate the process of removing them from the ground and decide where they should go. As I have said, it seems to me reasonable that the decision should be made by the government in whose soil they are found. But the right conclusion for them is not obviously that they should always stay exactly where they lay. Many

Egyptians—overwhelmingly Muslims who regard the religion of the pharaohs as idolatrous—nevertheless insist that all the antiquities ever exported from its borders are really theirs. You do not need to endorse Napoleon's depredations of North Africa to think that there is something to be said for allowing people in other countries the chance to see close up the arts of one of the world's great civilizations. And it's a painful irony that one reason we've lost information about cultural antiquities is the very regulation intended to preserve it. If, for example, I sell you a figure from Djenné-Jeno with evidence that it came out of the ground in a certain place after the regulations came into force, then I am giving the authorities in the United States, who are committed to the restitution of objects taken illegally out of Mali, the very evidence they need.

Suppose that, from the beginning, Mali had been encouraged and helped by UNESCO to exercise its trusteeship of these Djenné-Jeno terra-cottas by licensing digs and training people to recognize that objects removed carefully from the earth with accurate records of location are worth more, even to collectors, than objects without this essential element of provenance. Suppose they had required that objects be recorded and registered before leaving, and stipulated that if the national museum wished to keep an object, it would have to pay a market price for it; the acquisition fund being supported by a tax on the price of the exported objects. The digs encouraged by this regime would have been worse than proper, professionally conducted digs by accredited archaeologists. Some people would still have avoided the rules. But mightn't all this have been better than what actually happened? Suppose, further, that the Malians had decided that, in order to maintain and build their collections, they should auction off some works they own. The cultural-patrimony crowd, instead of praising them for committing needed resources to protecting the national collection, would have excoriated them for betraying their heritage.

The problem for Mali is not that it doesn't have enough Malian art. The problem is that it doesn't have enough money. In the short run, allowing Mali to stop the export of a good deal of the art in its territory does have the positive effect of making sure that there is some world-class art in Mali for Malians to experience. (This doesn't work well everywhere, since another feature of poor countries is that it's hard to stop valuable materials from disappearing from national collections and reappearing in international auction houses. That's especially true if the objects are poorly cataloged and worth many times the total annual salaries of the museum staff; which explains what has happened in Nigeria.) But an experience limited to Malian art—or, anyway, art made on territory that's now part of Mali—makes no more sense for a Malian than for anyone else. New technologies mean that Malians can now see, in however imperfectly reproduced a form, great art from around the planet. If UNESCO had spent as much effort to make it possible for great art to get into Mali as it has done to stop great art from getting out, it would have been serving better the interests that Malians, like all people, have in a cosmopolitan aesthetic experience.

Living with Art

How would the concept of cultural patrimony apply to cultural objects whose current owners acquired them legally in the normal way? You live in Norway. You buy a painting from a young, unknown artist named Edvard Munch. Your friends think it rather strange, but they get used to seeing it in your living room. Eventually, you leave it to your daughter. Time passes. Tastes change. The painting is now recognized as being the work of a major Norwegian artist, part of Norway's cultural patrimony. If that means that it literally belongs to Norway, then presumably the Norwegian government, on behalf of the people of Norway, should take it from her. After all, on this way of thinking, *it's theirs.* You live in Ibadan, in the heart of Yorubaland in Nigeria. It's the early sixties. You buy a painted carving from a guy—an actor, painter, sculptor, all-around artist—who calls himself Twin Seven Seven. Your family thinks it's a strange way to spend money. But once more time passes, and he comes to be seen as one of Nigeria's most important modern artists. More cultural patrimony for Nigeria, right? And if it's Nigeria's, it's not yours. So why can't the Nigerian government just take it, as the natural trustees of the Nigerian people, whose property it is?

Neither the Norwegians nor the Nigerians would in fact exercise their power in this way. (When antiquities are involved, though, a number of states will do so.) They are also committed, after all, to the idea of private property. Of course, if you were interested in selling, they might provide the resources for a public museum to buy it from you (though the government of Nigeria, at least, probably thinks it has more pressing calls on its treasury). So far, cultural property is just like any other property. Suppose, though, the governments didn't want to pay. There's something else they could do. If you sold your artwork, and the buyer, whatever his nationality, wanted to take the painting out of Norway or Nigeria, they could refuse permission to export it. The effect of the international regulations is to say that Norwegian cultural patrimony can be kept in Norway, Nigerian in Nigeria. An Italian law (passed, by the way, under Mussolini) permits the Italian government to deny export to any artwork over fifty years old currently owned by an Italian, even, presumably, if it's a Jasper Johns painting of the American flag. But, then, most countries require export licenses for significant cultural property (generally excepting the work of living artists). So much for being the cultural patrimony of humankind.

These cases are particularly troublesome, because neither

Munch nor Twin Seven Seven would have been the creator that he was if he'd been unaware of and unaffected by the work of artists in other places. If the argument for cultural patrimony is that the art belongs to the culture that gives it its significance, most art doesn't belong to a national culture at all. Much of the greatest art is flamboyantly international; much ignores nationality altogether. Early modern European art was court art, or it was church art. It was made not for nations or peoples but for princes or popes or *ad majorem gloriam dei*. And the artists who made it came from all over Europe. More importantly, in the line often ascribed to Picasso, good artists copy, great ones steal; and they steal from everywhere. Does Picasso himself—a Spaniard—get to be part of the cultural patrimony of the Republic of the Congo, home of the Vili, one of whose carvings the Frenchman Matisse showed him at the home of the American Gertrude Stein?

The problem was already there in the preamble to the 1954 Hague Convention that I quoted a little while back: ". . . *each people* makes its contribution to the culture of the world." That sounds like whenever someone makes a contribution, his or her "people" makes a contribution, too. And there's something odd, to my mind, about thinking of Hindu temple sculpture or Michelangelo's and Raphael's frescos in the Vatican as the contribution of a people, rather than the contribution of the individuals who made (and, if you like, paid for) them. I know that Michelangelo made a contribution to the culture of the world. I've gazed in wonder at the ceiling of the Sistine Chapel. I will grant that Their Holinesses Popes Julius II, Leo X, Clement VIII, and Paul III, who paid him, made a contribution, too. But which *people* exactly made that contribution? The people of the Papal States? The people of Michelangelo's native Caprese? The Italians?

This is clearly the wrong way to think about the matter. The right way is to take not a national but a cosmopolitan perspective: to ask what system of international rules about objects of this sort will respect the many legitimate human interests at stake. The point of many sculptures and paintings, the reason they were made and bought, was that they should be looked at and lived with. Each of us has an interest in being able, should we choose, to live with art; and that interest is not limited to the art of our own "people." Now, if an object acquires a wider significance, as part, say, of the oeuvre of a major artist, then other people will have a more substantial interest in being able to experience it and to the knowledge derived from its study. The object's aesthetic value is not fully captured by its value as private property. So you might think there was a case for giving people an incentive to share it. In America such incentives abound. You can get a tax deduction by giving a painting to a museum. You get social kudos for lending your artworks to shows, where they can be labeled "from the collection of . . ." And, finally, where an object is a masterpiece, you can earn a good sum by selling it at auction, while both allowing the curious a temporary window of access and providing for a new owner the pleasures you have already known. If it is good to share art in these ways with others, the cosmopolitan asks, why should the sharing cease at national borders?

In the spirit of cosmopolitanism, you might wonder whether all the greatest art should be held in trusteeship by nations, made widely available, shared across borders through traveling exhibitions, and in books and Web sites. Well, there's something to be said for the exhibitions and the books and the Web sites. There is no good reason, however, to think that public ownership is the ideal fate of every important art object. Much contemporary art— not just paintings, but conceptual artworks, sound sculptures, and a great deal more—was made for museums, designed for public display. But paintings, photographs, and sculptures, wherever they were created and whoever imagined them into being, have become one of the fundamental presences in the lives of millions of people. Is it really a sensible definition of great art that it is art that is too important to allow anybody to live with?

Culture™

Talk of "cultural property," even when directed at imperialism, has had imperial tendencies of its own. In recent years, various people have urged us to go further and take account of collective forms of *intellectual* property. The cause has been taken up by a number of anthropologists and legal experts and by spokesmen for indigenous groups as well. The Inter-Apache Summit on Repatriation, for example, claims tribal control over "all images, text, ceremonies, music, songs, stories, symbols, beliefs, customs, ideas and other physical and spiritual objects and concepts." A UN body circulates a Draft Declaration on the Rights of Indigenous Peoples (1994) affirming their right "to maintain, protect and develop the past, present and future manifestations of their cultures," including "artefacts, designs, ceremonies, technologies and visual and performing arts and literature, as well as the right to the restitution of cultural, intellectual, religious and spiritual property taken without their free and informed consent or in violation of their laws, traditions and customs." The World Intellectual Property Organization assembles a committee to explore how expressions of folklore can be given legal protections. A Mataatua Declaration proposes an expansion of the "cultural and intellectual property rights regime," given that "indigenous peoples are the guardians of their customary knowledge and have the right to protect and control dissemination of that knowledge," while the Julayinbul Statement on Indigenous Intellectual Property Rights declares that "Aboriginal intellectual property, within Aboriginal Common

Law, is an inherent inalienable right which cannot be terminated, extinguished or taken." As the anthropologist Michael F. Brown observes, in a discussion of these developments, "if native knowledge is held to be collective and eternal rather than the invention of a solitary author, then it follows that time limitations keyed to the human life span, which clearly reflect the possessive individualism of Western capitalist thought, should be replaced by some form of perpetual copyright."[4]

Notice what happens when we shift from tangible artifacts to intellectual property. It's no longer just a particular object but any reproducible image of it that must be regulated by those whose patrimony it is. We find ourselves obliged, in theory, to repatriate ideas and experiences. Epic poems—and there are still bards who recite them in Senegal, say, and parts of South India—would similarly be protected: reproduction prohibited without permission. So, too, with tunes and rhythms handed down over the generations. Brown notes that Zia Pueblo sought damages from New Mexico for having reproduced the Zia sun symbol on its license plates and flags. (No damages were paid, but a formal statement of apology was issued.) And matters get even more complicated when a group's ritual secrets are involved.

It all seems to follow from the logic of cultural patrimony. But the movement to confer the gleaming, new protections of intellectual property on such traditional practices would damage, irreparably, the nature of what it seeks to protect. For protection, here, involves partition, making countless mine-and-thine distinctions. And given the inevitably mongrel, hybrid nature of living cultures, it's doubtful that such an attempt could go very far. Not that we should we be eager to embark on it. For one thing, we've been poorly served by intellectual-property law when it comes to contemporary culture: software, stories, songs. All too often, laws have focused tightly on the interests of owners, often corporate owners, while the interests of consumers—of audiences, readers, viewers, and listeners—drop from sight. Talk of cultural patrimony ends up embracing the sort of hyper-stringent doctrine of property rights (property fundamentalism, Lawrence Lessig calls it) that we normally associate with international capital: the Disney Corporation, for instance, which would like to own Mickey Mouse in perpetuity.[5] It's just that the corporations that the patrimonialists favor are cultural groups. In the name of authenticity, they would extend this peculiarly Western, and modern, conception of ownership to every corner of the earth. The vision is of a cultural landscape consisting of Disney Inc. and the Coca-Cola Company, for sure; but also of Ashanti Inc., Navajo Inc., Maori Inc., Norway Inc.: All rights reserved.

Human Interest

When we're trying to interpret the concept of cultural property, we ignore at our peril what lawyers, at least, know: property is an institution, created largely by laws which are best designed by thinking about how they can serve the human interests of those whose behavior they govern. If the laws are international laws, then they govern everyone. And the human interests in question are the interests of all of humankind. However self-serving it may seem, the British Museum's claim to be a repository of the heritage not of Britain but of the world seems to me exactly right. Part of the obligation, though, will be to make those collections ever more widely available not just in London but elsewhere, through traveling collections, through publications, and through the World Wide Web.

It has been too easy to lose sight of the global constituency. The legal scholar John Henry Merryman has offered a litany of examples of how laws and treaties relating to cultural property have betrayed a properly cosmopolitan (he uses the word "internationalist") perspective. "Any cultural internationalist would oppose the removal of monumental sculptures from Mayan sites where physical damage or the loss of artistic integrity or cultural information would probably result, whether the removal was illegally or legally, but incompetently, done," he writes. "The same cultural internationalist, however, might wish that Mexico would sell or trade or lend some of its reputedly large hoard of unused *Chac-Mols*, pots and other objects to foreign collectors or museums." And though we readily deplore the theft of paintings from Italian churches, "if a painting is rotting in a church from lack of resources to care for it, and the priest sells it for money to repair the roof and in the hope that the purchaser will give the painting the care it needs, then the problem begins to look different."[6]

So when I lament the modern thefts from Nigerian museums or Malian archaeological sites or the imperial ones from Asante, it's because the property rights that were trampled upon in these cases flow from laws that I think are reasonable. I am not for sending every object "home." Much Asante art now in Europe, America, and Japan was sold or given by people who had the right to alienate them under the laws that then prevailed, laws that, as I say, were perfectly reasonable. The mere fact that something you own is important to the descendants of people who gave it away does not generally give them an entitlement to it. (Even less should you return it to people who don't want it because a committee in Paris has declared it their patrimony.) It is a fine gesture to return things to the descendants of their makers—or to offer it to them for sale— but it certainly isn't a duty. You might also show your respect for the culture it came from by holding on to it because you value it yourself. Furthermore, because cultural property has a value for all of us, it can be reasonable to insist that those to whom it is returned are in a position to take trusteeship; repatriation of some objects to poor countries whose priorities cannot be with their museum budgets might just lead to their decay. Were I advising a poor community pressing for the return of many ritual objects, I might urge it to consider whether leaving some of them to be respectfully displayed in other countries might not be part of its contribution to the cosmopolitan enterprise of cross-cultural understanding as well as a way to ensure their survival for later generations.

To be sure, there are various cases where repatriation makes sense. We won't, however, need the concept of cultural patrimony to understand them. Consider, for example, objects whose meaning would be deeply enriched by being returned to the context from which they were taken; site-specific art of one kind and another. Here there is an aesthetic argument for return. Or take objects of contemporary ritual significance that were acquired legally from people around the world in the course of European colonial expansion. If an object is central to the cultural or religious life of the members of a community, there *is* a human reason for it to find its place back with them. The communities in question are almost never national communities; still, the states within which they lie may be their natural representatives in negotiating their return. Such cases are bound to be messy: it will often be unclear if a work is site-specific or how an outsider should judge whether something is central to a community's religious life. Law, whether national or international, may well not be the best way to settle these questions.

But the clearest cases for repatriation are those where objects were stolen from people whose names we often know—people whose heirs, like the king of Asante, would like them back. As someone who grew up in Kumasi, I confess I was pleased when some of this stolen art was returned, thus enriching the new palace museum for locals and for tourists. (Thank you, Prince Charles.) Still, I don't think we should demand everything back, even everything that was stolen; not least because we haven't the remotest chance of getting it. Don't waste your time insisting on getting what you can't get. There must be an Akan proverb with that message.

There is, however, a more important reason: I actually want museums in Europe to be able to show the riches of the society they plundered in the years when my grandfather was a young man. I'd rather that we negotiated as restitution not just the major objects of significance for our history, things that make the best sense in the palace museum at Manhyia, but a decent collection of art from around the world. Because perhaps the greatest of the many ironies of the sacking of Kumasi in 1874 is that it deprived my hometown of a collection that was, in fact, splendidly cosmopolitan. As Sir Garnet Wolseley prepared to loot and then blow up the Aban, the large stone building in the city's center, European and American journalists were allowed to wander through it. The British *Daily Telegraph* described it as "the museum, for museum it should be called, where the art treasures of the monarchy were stored." The London *Times*'s Winwood Reade wrote that each of its rooms "was a perfect Old Curiosity Shop." "Books in many languages," he continued, "Bohemian glass, clocks, silver plate, old furniture, Persian rugs, Kidderminster carpets, pictures and engravings, numberless chests and coffers. . . . With these were many specimens of Moorish and Ashantee handicraft." The *New York Herald* augmented the list: "yataghans and scimitars of Arabic make, Damask bed-curtains and counterpanes, English engravings, an oil painting of a gentleman, an old uniform of a West Indian soldier, brass blunderbusses, prints from illustrated newspapers, and, among much else, copies of the London *Times* . . . for 17 October 1843."

We shouldn't become overly sentimental about these matters. Many of the treasures in the Aban were no doubt war booty as well. Still, it will be a long time before Kumasi has a collection as rich both in our own material culture and in works from other places as those destroyed by Sir Garnet Wolseley and the founder of the Boy Scouts. The Aban had been completed in 1822. It was a prize project of the Asantehene Osei Bonsu, who had apparently been impressed by what he'd heard about the British Museum.[7]

Imaginary Connections

Cosmopolitanism, as we've been conceiving it, starts with what is human in humanity. So we understand the urge to bring these objects "home." We, too, feel what Walter Benjamin called the "aura" of the work of art, which has to do with its uniqueness, its singularity. In this age of mechanical reproduction, Benjamin noticed, where we can make good facsimiles of anything, the original has only increased in value. It is relatively easy nowadays to make a copy of the Mona Lisa so good that merely looking at it— as you would look at the original in the Louvre—you could not tell the copy from the original. But only the original has the aura: only it has the connection with the hand of Leonardo. That is why millions of people, who could have spent their plane fare on buying a great reproduction, have been to the Louvre. They want the aura. It is a kind of magic; and it is the same kind of magic that nations feel toward their history. A Norwegian thinks of the Norsemen as her ancestors. She wants not just to know what their swords look like but to stand close to an actual sword, wielded in actual battles, forged by a particular smith. Some of the heirs to the kingdom of Benin, the people of Southwest Nigeria, want the bronze their ancestors cast, shaped, handled, wondered at. They would like to wonder at—if we will not let them touch—that very thing. The connection people feel to cultural objects that are symbolically theirs, because they were produced from within a world of meaning created by their ancestors—the connection to art through identity—is powerful. It should be acknowledged. The cosmopolitan, though, wants to remind us of other connections.

One connection—the one neglected in talk of cultural patrimony—is the connection not *through* identity but *despite* difference. We can respond to art that is not ours; indeed, we can fully respond to "our" art only if we move beyond thinking of it as ours and start to respond to it as art. But equally important is the human connection. My people—human beings—made the Great Wall of China, the Chrysler Building, the Sistine Chapel: these things were made by creatures like me, through the exercise of skill and imagination. I do not have those skills, and my imagination spins different dreams. Nevertheless, that potential is also in me. The connection through a local identity is as imaginary as the connection through humanity. The Nigerian's link to the Benin bronze, like mine, is a connection made in the imagination; but to say this isn't to pronounce either of them unreal. They are among the realest connections that we have.

CHAPTER 9

THE COUNTER-COSMOPOLITANS

Believers without Borders

They believe in human dignity across the nations, and they live their creed. They share these ideals with people in many countries, speaking many languages. As thoroughgoing globalists, they make full use of the World Wide Web. This band of brothers and sisters resists the crass consumerism of modern Western society and its growing influence in the rest of the world. But these people also resist the temptations of the narrow nationalisms of the countries where they were born. They would never go to war *for* a country; but they will enlist in a campaign *against* any nation that gets in the way of universal justice. Indeed, they resist the call of all local allegiances, all traditional loyalties, even to family. They oppose them because they get in the way of the one thing that matters: building a community of enlightened men and women across the

world. That is one reason they also reject traditional religious authorities (though they also disapprove of their obscurantism and tem-
porizing). Not that they think of themselves as antireligious. Far
from it; but their faith is simple and clear and direct. Sometimes,
they agonize in their discussions about whether they can reverse
the world's evils or whether their struggle is hopeless. But mostly they
soldier on in their efforts to make the world a better place.

These are not the secret heirs to the Cynic cosmopolitans,
whose cause, too, was global, because they, too, had no time for
the local and the customary. The community these comrades are
building is not a *polis*; they call it the *ummah*, the community of the
faithful, and it is open to all who share their faith. They are young,
global Muslim fundamentalists; they are the recruiting grounds
for Al Qaeda.

Though some of them are Americans, the division they make
between faithful and infidel is not one most Americans would recognize. Many people one would normally say were Muslims—
because they call themselves Muslim, declare that God is one and
Mahomet his Prophet, pray daily to Mecca, give charity, even make
the hajj—are on the outside of their community, in urgent need
of being returned to the true faith. The *ummah*'s new globalists
consider that they have returned to the fundamentals of Islam;
much of what passes for Islam in the world, much of what has
passed as Islam for centuries, they think a sham. As the French
scholar Olivier Roy writes in his superb account of the phenome-
non, *Globalized Islam*,

> Of course, by definition Islam is universal, but after the time of
> the Prophet and his companions (the Salaf) it has always been
> embedded in given cultures. These cultures seem now a mere
> product of history and the results of many influences and idio-
> syncrasies. For fundamentalists (and also for some liberals) there

is nothing in these cultures to be proud of, because they have altered the pristine message of Islam. Globalization is a good opportunity to dissociate Islam from any given culture and to provide a model that could work beyond any culture.[1]

In their rejection of traditional religious authorities and their reliance on their own interpretations of the Koran and the traditions of their faith, they are, in many ways, like Christian fundamentalists in the United States. They, too, think that churches and scholars often get between the Bible and the faithful, that Holy Scripture can speak very well for itself. The new Muslim fundamentalists—neofundamentalists, Roy calls them—typically communicate in English because many of them grew up in parts of the world, including Europe and North America, where Arabic is not spoken, and this global language, which is also understood by many educated Muslims in Egypt, Pakistan, or Malaysia, is the one they have in common. (So they share with most Christian fundamentalists their ignorance of the original languages of the Scriptures they interpret.) Most Islamic theory about relations between Muslims and non-Muslims was developed over the centuries in Muslim countries to deal with non-Muslim minorities; but a third of the world's Muslims now live in countries that have non-Muslim majorities. Indeed, as Olivier Roy so elegantly demonstrates, globalized Islam is in part a response to the experience of Muslims as minorities.

They may be the children of Algerian immigrants in France or of Bengali or Pakistani immigrants in England; they may be from Turkey or Saudi Arabia or Sudan or Zanzibar or Malaysia. Islam for them is fundamentally a faith, a set of practices (prayer and fasting, charity, the hajj, but also eating halal meat and avoiding alcohol), and a commitment to certain values—like cleanliness and modesty—in daily life. Such neofundamentalists may speak of Muslim culture. But they largely reject the culture within which their religion was embedded in the places their Muslim ancestors came from. That culture is treated skeptically, Roy says, as "a mere product of history." They have taken a religion that came with a form of life and thrown away much of the form of life. They have no need of national loyalties or cultural traditions.

Now, the vast majority of these, mostly young, neofundamentalists are not going to blow anybody up. So they should not be confused with those other Muslims—Roy calls them the "radical neofundamentalists"—who want to turn jihad, interpreted as literal warfare against the West, into the sixth pillar of Islam. But there are fundamentalists whose aversion to terrorism and violence is as profound as bin Ladin's dedication to it. Whether to endorse the use of violence is a political decision, even if it's to be justified in religious terms. And, indeed, Roy thinks that the failure of jihad— Osama bin Ladin's failure—may have turned many fundamentalists back to *dawa*—preaching and precept, exhortation and example—as the right way to bring outsiders in and apostates back to the faith.

What is happening within Islam, especially outside the Muslim countries, is parallel to similar phenomena that are going on among the Christians next door. We see, as Roy observes, the same "quest for a universal community beyond cultures and nations"; and in both cases a "move toward the individualization of religion."[2] And this newly individualized Islam is, like Catholic or Protestant versions of fundamentalism, perfectly consistent with political and social integration as a minority within the framework of a democratic republic that allows freedom of religion.

What distinguishes the neofundamentalists, violent or not, is that they exemplify the possibility of a kind of universal ethics that inverts the picture of cosmopolitanism I've been elaborating. Universalism without toleration, it's clear, turns easily to murder. This is one lesson we can learn from the sad history of Christian religious warfare in Europe. The universalist principle *un roi, une foi, une loi* (one king, one faith, one law) underlay the French Wars of Religion that bloodied the four decades before the Edict of Nantes of 1598, in which Henri IV of France finally granted to the Protestants in his realm the right to practice their faith. In the Thirty Years' War, which ravaged central Europe until 1648 and the Peace of Westphalia, Protestant and Catholic princes from Austria to Sweden struggled with one another, and hundreds of thousands of Germans died in battle. Millions starved or died of disease as roaming armies pillaged the countryside. In the English Civil War, between 1639 and 1651, which pitted Protestant armies against the forces of a Catholic king, perhaps as many as 10 percent of the inhabitants of England, Scotland, Wales, and Ireland died in warfare or the disease and starvation that came in the aftermath of battle. In all these conflicts, issues beyond sectarian doctrine were always, no doubt, at stake. But many Enlightenment liberals drew the conclusion that insisting on one vision of universal truth could only lead the world back to the bloodbaths. It was a lesson drawn equally by many in the West who railed against the Inquisition: again, cruelty conducted, as so often, in the name of moral cleansing, murder in the name of universal truth.

Intolerance of religious difference in the Christian world is not, I hasten to say, only a thing of the past. Many American Christians believe that atheists, Jews, Muslims, Buddhists, and the rest will go to hell unless they accept Jesus Christ. There are Protestants who think this about other Protestants; some who think it about Catholics and, no doubt, vice versa. This is a view that can, perhaps, be held with a compassion that will lead you to want to convert those whose eternal fates hang so precariously in the balance; but it is not one that necessarily leads to respect for those who are living in error. Among our Christian fellow citizens, there are some, though not, I think, very many, who want to make our government and society more Christian, with the Ten Commandments in every courthouse, abortion and homosexuality proscribed, evolution off the biology syllabus. But that is usually about it. The centuries of massacre by Christian princes and the Holy Office are long gone.

Still, we should remember that there have been Christian terrorists in the United States and that one of them, Eric Rudolph, has been convicted of leaving a large pipe bomb in a park in Atlanta during the 1996 Olympic Games, which killed a woman named Alice Hawthorne, injured more than a hundred other people, and would, but for the prompt action of a security guard, have killed and injured many more. Attacking the Olympics is about as straightforward a way as there is of declaring yourself an enemy of cosmopolitanism's conversation across the nations. Rudolph has also been convicted of killing an off-duty police officer at a clinic in Birmingham where abortions were sometimes performed and with bombing a lesbian bar in Atlanta. These are more than suggestions that he shares the aims, though not (need I insist?) the usual methods, of the Christian right. As news reports suggest, what's especially troubling is the amount of support that Rudolph seems to have enjoyed in places like Murphy, North Carolina, where he was finally apprehended. Many of its residents openly identified with Rudolph; during the police manhunt, bumper stickers and T-shirts with the slogan "Run, Rudolph, Run" were printed and sold by local businesses. "Rudolph's a Christian and I'm a Christian and he dedicated his life to fighting abortion," a young woman from Murphy, a mother of four, told a *New York Times* reporter. "Those are our values. These are our woods. I don't see what he did as a terrorist act."[3]

Timothy McVeigh killed 168 men, women, and children, when he bombed the Alfred P. Murrah Federal Building in Oklahoma City; and though his motive seems to have had nothing to do with religion, he is a hero of some in the Christian Identity movement, which grounds its hatred of black people and Jews and the federal government in something they apparently believe is a form of Christianity. I am not equating these crimes to the multinational murder spree whose guiding spirit is Osama bin Ladin. There's no question that he and various groups more or less loosely affiliated with or inspired by him pose the greatest danger of terrorism against the United States; and that the popularity Osama enjoys among the counter-cosmopolitans makes him a far from marginal figure. But it is easier for us to remember that Osama bin Ladin is not the typical Muslim when we recall that Eric Rudolph is not the typical Christian.

They are not parallel in another way. So far as I am aware, no large organized Christian terror network is planning attacks on Muslim countries or institutions. There are many reasons for that, I think. One of them is surely that very few Christians see Islam as posing a threat to their way of life. Why many Muslims *do* feel that Christians are still engaged in a crusade against them is a complicated question. I am inclined to agree with those who think that an important element in the psychological mix is a sense that Islam, which once led Christendom, has somehow fallen behind, a sense that produces an uncomfortable mélange of resentment, anger, envy, and admiration.

But to offer explanations for such counter-cosmopolitanism still doesn't address the conceptual challenge it poses to those of us who believe in moral universals: how, in principle, to distinguish benign and malign forms of universalism?

Competing Universalities

I mentioned tolerance. Yet there are plenty of things that the heroes of radical Islam are happy to tolerate. They don't care if you eat kebabs or meatballs or kung pao chicken, as long as the meat is halal; your hijab can be silk or linen or viscose. On the other hand, there are limits to cosmopolitan tolerance. We will sometimes want to intervene in other places, because what is going on there violates our fundamental principles so deeply. We, too, can see moral error. And when it is serious enough—genocide is the uncontroversial case—we will not stop with conversation. Toleration requires a concept of the *in*tolerable.

Then, as I said at the start, we cosmopolitans believe in universal truth, too, though we are less certain that we have it all already. It is not skepticism about the very idea of truth that guides us; it is realism about how hard the truth is to find. One truth we hold to, however, is that every human being has obligations to every other. Everybody matters: that is our central idea. And it sharply limits the scope of our tolerance.

To say what, in principle, distinguishes the cosmopolitan from the counter-cosmopolitan, we plainly need to go beyond talk of truth and tolerance. One distinctively cosmopolitan commitment is to *pluralism*. Cosmopolitans think that there are many values worth living by and that you cannot live by all of them. So we hope and expect that different people and different societies will embody different values. (But they have to be values *worth* living by.) Another aspect of cosmopolitanism is what philosophers call *fallibilism*—the sense that our knowledge is imperfect, provisional, subject to revision in the face of new evidence.

The neofundamentalist conception of a global *ummah*, by contrast, admits of local variations—but only in matters that don't matter. These counter-cosmopolitans, once more like many Christian fundamentalists, do think that there is one right way for all human beings to live; that all the differences must be in the details. If your concern is global homogeneity, this utopia, not the world that capitalism is producing, is the one that you should worry about. Still, the universalisms in the name of religion are hardly the only ones that invert the cosmopolitan creed. In the name of universal humanity, you can be the kind of Marxist, like Mao or Pol Pot, who wants to eradicate all religion, just as easily as you can be the Grand Inquisitor supervising an auto-da-fé. Their mirror is not shattered, it is whole: and we have no shard of it. All of these men want everyone on their side, so we can share with them the vision in their mirror. "Indeed, I'm a trustworthy adviser to you," Osama bin Laden said in a 2002 "message to the American people." "I invite you to the happiness of this world and the hereafter and to escape your dry, miserable, materialistic life that is without soul. I invite you to Islam, that calls to follow of the path of Allah alone Who has no partners, the path which calls for justice and forbids oppression and crimes." Join us, the counter-cosmopolitans say, and we will all be sisters and brothers. But each of them plans to trample on our differences—to trample us to death, if necessary—if we will not join them. Their motto might as well be that sardonic German saying:

> Und willst du nicht mein Bruder sein,
>   So schlag' ich Dir den Schädel ein.
> *If you don't want to be my brother,*
>   *Then I'll smash your skull in.*

For the counter-cosmopolitans, then, universalism issues in uniformity. The cosmopolitan may be happy to abide by the Golden Rule about doing onto others (putting aside, for the moment, the conceptual problems of "universalizability" I discussed earlier). But cosmopolitans care if those others don't *want* to be done unto as I would be done unto. It's not necessarily the end of the matter, but it's something we think we need to take account of. Our understanding of toleration means interacting on terms of respect with those who see the world differently. We cosmopolitans think we might learn something even from those we disagree with. We think people have a right to their own lives.

In some of the pronunciamentos of radical Islam, in turn, you find that such conversation across differences is exactly what is to be shunned. Here, for example, is a message from Dr. Aymen al-Zawahiri, a longtime associate of Osama bin Ladin's, translated from a tape released on February 11, 2005, and circulated on the Web by his admirers:

> The Sharee'ah brought down by Allah is the Sharee'ah which must be followed. In this matter, no person is able to stand in a position of waviness or oscillation; it is a matter that can only be received very seriously because it doesn't accept jokes. Either you are a believer in Allah and then you have to abide by His laws, or you are a disbeliever in Him, and then there is no use in discussing with you the details of His law. The waviness which western secularism desires to spread, no proper mind which respects itself can accept. Because Allah if he is the Ruler then He has the right to rule; this is obvious and there is no hesitation. . . .
>
> And so it is that if you are a disbeliever in Allah, then logically there is no use in debating with you the details of His laws.

The fear of conversation here is evidently propelled by a concern that exchanges with people of different views could lead the faithful astray. There is no curiosity about the ways of the "disbeliever." All we are is embodiments of error.

But, of course, many Muslims—including many religious scholars—have debated the nature of sharia, or Islamic religious law. Over the last two centuries, one can identify distinguished Islamic scholars who have engaged seriously with ideas from outside Islam. In the nineteenth century, Sayyid Ahmad Khan in India and

Muhammad 'Adbuh in Egypt both sought to develop Muslim visions of modernity. More recently, Mahmud Muhammad Taha in Sudan, Tariq Ramadan in Europe, and Khaled Abou El-Fadl in the United States have all developed their views in dialogue with the non-Muslim world. These Muslim thinkers are wildly different, but each of them challenges—and with a far more extensive ground-ing in the corpus of earlier Muslim scholarship than al-Zawahiri—the fundamentalist conceptions of sharia.[4] Ahmed al-Tayeb, president of Al-Azhar, the world's oldest Muslim university (in fact, the oldest university, period), has invited the archbishop of Canterbury to speak from his pulpit. And he has said, "God created diverse peoples. Had He wanted to create a single *ummah*, He would have, but He chose to make them different until the day of resurrection. Every Muslim must fully understand this principle. A relationship based on conflict is futile."[5] Insofar as they think there is something to discuss, al-Zawahiri's syllogism decrees all these men to be "disbelievers."

It is pointless, I think, for those of us who are not Muslims to say what is real and what is ersatz Islam; just as it would be inane for al-Zawahiri to weigh in on whether, say, contraception or cap-ital punishment is consistent with Christianity. It is up to those who want to sail under the flags of Christianity or of Islam to deter-mine (and explain, if they wish to) what their banners mean. That is their fight. But among those who call themselves Muslims, there are more tolerant exponents and there have been more tolerant times. We can observe the historical fact that there have been soci-eties that called themselves Muslim and practiced toleration (includ-ing, in the every earliest period, under the command of the Prophet himself). So it is heartening, at least for a cosmopolitan, that there are now many Muslim voices speaking for religious toleration and arguing for it from within the interpretative traditions of Islam.

Eid al-Fitr with the Safis

I wasn't raised a Muslim, but I was raised among Muslims. My sense of Islam, therefore, begins with family memories; and, like so many childhood memories, the mise-en-scène is the dinner table. When I was a child, we often visited our Muslim cousins, the Safis, for dinner and the food (and the company) was always something to look forward to. But I looked forward especially to the feasting on Eid al-Fitr, the feast that starts on the last day of Ramadan, once the sun has set. Ramadan is a month of daylong fasts. As they fast, Muslims recall the origins of the Koran, which they believe was given to the Prophet Muhammad by God, beginning in this ninth month of the Muslim calendar. Between sunrise and sunset, devout Muslims eat and drink nothing. Many will go to mosque to hear the Holy Koran being read. Then, in the evening, they come together for a family meal to break the daily fast. On the last day of the month, at the festival of Eid, there is this last, great feast; the climax of the celebration, the end of the fast.

Auntie Grace, my father's cousin, supervised the cooking. She was, as it happens, a Christian, and she was not an Asante but a Fanti from the coast. But she had married Uncle Aviv, a Lebanese businessman who had settled in Kumasi many years before, and she had learned to cook Lebanese food—as she cooked traditional Ghanaian dishes—to perfection. There was hummus and tabbouleh, falafel and baba ghanoush, kibbeh and *loubia*, followed by delicious sweet pastries, fresh fruit, and strong, dark, sweet coffee.

I loved Auntie Grace's cooking. And, especially later in my childhood, after I'd been sent to an English boarding school, I too often found I was the last one still eating, seated in front of a plate with Uncle Aviv at my side, gently adding another kibbeh—the oval patties of lamb and *burghul*—or spooning a few more of the green beans in tomato sauce, the *loubia*, onto my plate. Eventually, defeated, I would tell him I could eat no more. At my boarding school, I had been taught that you must eat everything that was served to you. (Forty years on, I still recall spending an excruciating half an hour after lunch one day at school while the matron forced me to finish some fatty boiled beef.) But in Uncle Aviv's gastronomic tradition—a generous Arab tradition in which hospitality is central—the guest is satisfied only if he leaves something on the plate. It took me a while to sort through these two different systems of etiquette, but I learned, in the end, that if I wanted to keep from being uncomfortably full, I would have to breach the customs of my mother's country when I was eating with my uncle from Lebanon.

If we had been living in America, I suspect that at some point it would have seemed necessary to explain to us Christian cousins the significance of Ramadan. But we were in Ghana, a country where Christians, Muslims, and the followers of traditional religions live side by side, accepting each other's different ways without expressing much curiosity about them. Auntie Grace went to church on Sundays during Ramadan, as usual. Our cousins came to us at Christmas. I feasted in Ramadan throughout my childhood, but I learned what it meant only when I read about it for myself as an adult.

Muhammad himself, according to the Koran, had friendly relations with the Jews and Christians of Arabia (and when he fought them, it wasn't about matters of faith). He seems to have thought of the Koran as a special revelation for the Arabs from the one God who had made the covenant with the children of Israel and sent Jesus to the Christians. (This was more than a thousand years before the Roman Catholic Church—in Pope Paul VI's encyclical "Nostra Aetate"—declared that it regarded "with sincere reverence those ways of conduct and of life, those precepts and teachings which, though differing in many aspects from the ones she holds and sets forth, nonetheless often reflect a ray of that Truth which enlightens all men.") The Koran says,

> Be courteous when you argue with the People of the Book, except with those among them that do evil. Say: "We believe in that which has been revealed to you. Our God and your God is One. To Him we submit."

It also says, "There shall be no compulsion in religion."[6]

Not only the Koran but the practice of the Prophet, as reported in the Ahadith, does not require the conversion of the Ahl al-Kitab, the People of the Book (as the Koran calls Jews, Christians, and Zoroastrians). Beginning in the seventh century AD, the early caliphs, Muhammad's successors as rulers of the Muslim empire that exploded out of Arabia in the first century of Islam, took the largely Christian and Jewish communities they conquered under their protection without requiring conversion; in Persia, where they found not Jews or Christians but Zoroastrians, they extended the same courtesies to this other older tradition. When Akbar ruled his Muslim Empire in North India, he practiced the sort of toleration for the local Indian traditions that the early caliphs had shown for the People of the Book. He built Hindu temples and encouraged dialogue among scholars of all religions, including Sikhs, Buddhists, and Jains, along with Jews, Zoroastrians, various sects of Christians, and, indeed, various traditions of Islam.

I knew none of this when I was young. I knew only that my Uncle Aviv was a devout Muslim and that he was also tolerant and gentle. He came from a country riven by religious divides: among the Muslims, there are both Sunni and Shia communities, divided further among Alawites, Ismailis, Twelver Shias, and Druze; among the Christians, there are Roman, Armenian, and Syrian Catholics,

Greek, Armenian, and Syrian Orthodox, Chaldeans, Maronites, and a variety of Protestant denominations. Uncle Aviv, though, seemed to be equally open to people of all faiths. Perhaps that made him, by the standards of some of today's noisiest preachers of Islam, a bad Muslim. But it also made him quite typical of many Muslims in many nations and at many times. Indeed, Uncle Aviv would doubtless have felt that his form of Islam, being interwoven with the customs and practices he grew up in, was a richer, more sustaining faith than the thin abstractions of the rootless, individualistic zealots of neofundamentalism. Again, it's not for me to say. Still, though Muslims like him are less clamorous than the zealots, it's safe to venture that they are also more numerous.

Little Platoons

If cosmopolitanism is, in a slogan, universality plus difference, there is the possibility of another kind of enemy, one who rejects universality altogether. "Not everybody matters" would be their slogan. The fact is, though, that, whatever may have been the case in the past, most people who say it now don't really believe it. Bernard Williams wrote in *Ethics and the Limits of Philosophy* that "morality"—in the sense of norms that are universally binding—"is not an invention of philosophers. It is the outlook or, incoherently, part of the outlook of almost all of us."[7] Part of what he meant is that most people believe they have certain obligations that are, to use his word, inescapable. And one such inescapable obligation is this: when you do something that harms someone else, you must be able to justify it. Those we think of as willing to claim that not everyone matters—the Nazis, the racists, the chauvinists of one sort and another—don't stop with saying, "Those people don't matter." They tell you why. Jews are destroying our nation. Black people are inferior. Tutsi are cockroaches. The Aztecs are enemies of the faith. It's not that they don't matter; it's that they have *earned* our hatred or contempt. They deserve what we are doing to them.

This is what happens when you start to give reasons. Faced, especially, with an audience that includes some of those you are claiming do not matter, you are drawn into explaining, even to them, why you are going to do unto them what you would not have done unto you. Once you start defending your nation (or race or tribe), you will be drawn into explaining why your people's being on top is really better for everybody, even those you are abusing. So-called realists about international relations often say that our foreign policy should pursue only our own national interest. They *sound* as though they're saying that nobody matters but our own fellow countrymen. But if you ask them whether they think that we should engage in genocide if it is in our national interest, they typically deny that it *could* be in our national interest, because our national interest is somehow internally connected with certain values. To this line of response, I say, "Good. Then one of our values is that other people matter at least enough that we shouldn't kill them just because it suits us." Edmund Burke, that great defender of the local, is often quoted saying that "to love the little platoon we belong to in society, is the first principle (the germ as it were) of public affections." But here, too, the reason he offered appealed to universal considerations: "It is the first link in the series by which we proceed towards a love to our country and to mankind."[8]

I don't pretend that the reasons that people offer for ignoring the interests of strangers *explain* why people sometimes treat one another so badly. (As I've already said, I don't think that's how moral reasoning works.) And, of course, I don't think these reasons *justify* such bad behavior. Once you start offering reasons for ignoring the interests of others, however, reasoning itself will usually draw you into a kind of universality. A reason is an offer of a ground for thinking or feeling or doing something. And it isn't a ground for me, unless it's a ground for you. If someone really thinks that some group of people genuinely doesn't matter at all, he will suppose they are outside the circle of those to whom justifications are due. (That's one reason it's easier to think that animals don't matter than to think that people don't matter: animals can't ask us why we are abusing them.) Still, if people really do think some people don't matter at all, there is only one thing to do: try to change their minds, and, if you fail, make sure that they can't put their ideas into action.

The real challenge to cosmopolitanism isn't the belief that other people don't matter at all; it's the belief that they don't matter very much. It's easy to get agreement that we have *some* obligations to strangers. We can't do terrible things to them. Perhaps, if their situation becomes completely intolerable and we can do something about it at reasonable cost, we may even have a duty to intervene. Perhaps we should stop genocide, intervene when there is mass starvation or a great natural disaster. But must we do more than this? Here's where easy assent starts to fray.

I have been saying, in the name of the cosmopolitan ideal, that we have obligations to strangers. It is time, in closing, to say more about what those obligations are.

CHAPTER 10

KINDNESS TO STRANGERS

Killing the Mandarin

In Balzac's *Père Goriot*, there's a scene in which Eugène Rastignac, a young man tormented by social ambitions he lacks the means to support, is speaking to a medical-student friend about a question he attributes (wrongly, as it happens) to Rousseau:

> "Do you recall the passage where he asks the reader what he'd do if he could make himself rich by killing an old mandarin in China merely by willing it, without budging from Paris?"
>
> "Yes."
>
> "Well?"
>
> "Bah! I'm on my thirty-third mandarin."
>
> "Don't make a joke of it. Really, if it were proved to you that

the thing was possible and that a nod of your head would be enough, would you do it?"[1]

Rastignac's question is splendidly philosophical. Who but a philosopher would place magical murder in one pan of the scales and a million gold louis in the other? And, in fact, though Rousseau doesn't seem to have posed this question, Balzac might have been inspired by a passage from another eminent philosopher, the Scotsman Adam Smith. In *The Theory of Moral Sentiments* (1759), he writes memorably about the limits of the moral imagination. Smith's argument begins with an imagined earthquake swallowing up "the great empire of China." Surely a "man of humanity in Europe" would be moved to sorrow by news of the event and reflect on its melancholy meaning, perhaps even on its effects on world trade. Still, Smith says, once he had had these feelings and completed these reflections, he would return, untroubled, to his ordinary life. "The most frivolous disaster which could befal himself would occasion a more real disturbance," Smith wrote, and he went on,

> If he was to lose his little finger to-morrow, he would not sleep to-night; but, provided he never saw them, he will snore with the most profound security over the ruin of a hundred millions of his brethren. . . . To prevent, therefore, this paltry misfortune to himself, would a man of humanity be willing to sacrifice the lives of a hundred millions of his brethren, provided he had never seen them? Human nature startles with horror at the thought, and the world, in its greatest depravity and corruption, never produced such a villain as could be capable of entertaining it. But what makes this difference?

How is it, he wonders, that our "passive feelings" can be so selfish while our "active principles" are often so generous? "It is not the soft

power of humanity, it is not that feeble spark of benevolence which
Nature has lighted up in the human heart, that is thus capable of
counteracting the strongest impulses of self-love," he concludes.
"It is a stronger power, a more forcible motive, which exerts itself
upon such occasions. It is reason, principle, conscience, the inhabitant of the breast, the man within, the great judge and arbiter of
our conduct."[2]

Smith asks whether we would contemplate doing a great wrong
for a small benefit; Rastignac has us wondering whether we would
do a lesser wrong for a very great benefit. In shifting the example,
Balzac has moved from an exploration of moral psychology, which
was Smith's aim, to a question of basic morality. We'll do well to keep
both in mind. If we were to apportion our efforts to the strength of
our feelings, we would sacrifice a hundred millions to save our little finger (Smith's inference); and if we would do that (this is
Rastignac's corollary), we would surely sacrifice a single faraway
life to gain a great fortune. We know mandarins die everyday: what
grasp does that knowledge have on our feelings? That the test case
is China presupposes that, for those nearby, reason might not be
necessary. A Scotsman would presumably respond to destruction
of his fellow Scots not with reason but with passion. He doesn't
need reason. It is his ox that is being gored.

If you start with this thought, you will naturally ask whether
cosmopolitan talk of what we owe to strangers is likely to remain
a sonorous abstraction. "Cosmopolitanism as an ethical commitment strains to extend our concrete realities to include some dis-
tant and generalized 'others' who, we are told, are our global
neighbours," Robert Sibley has written. "The idea might give you
the warm-and-fuzzies, but it's nothing for which you'd be willing to
go to war."[3] What's presupposed here is that cosmopolitan moral
judgment requires us to feel about everyone in the world what we
feel about our literal neighbors (a strength of feeling that is per-

haps exaggerated by the suggestion that for them, at least, we would risk our lives). We can't be intimate with billions; ergo, we can't make the cosmopolitan judgment. But, as Adam Smith saw, to say that we have obligations to strangers isn't to demand that they have the same grip on our sympathies as our nearest and dearest. We'd better start with the recognition that they don't.

Taking Smith's answer seriously, though, requires that our cosmopolitanism should not make impossible psychological demands. Robert Sibley's skepticism is a natural response, I think, to some of the demands that moral cosmopolitans have recently made. So how much do we really owe to strangers?

The Shallow Pond

Here's one answer. "To behave in a way that's not seriously wrong, a well-off person, like you and me, must contribute to vitally effective groups, like OXFAM and UNICEF, most of the money and property she now has, and most of what comes her way for the foreseeable future": that's what the philosopher Peter Unger has argued, in a book provocatively entitled *Living High and Letting Die.*[4]

I've cut to the chase. But philosophers have defended such a view in considerable detail. One of Unger's points of departure is a famous analogy previously offered by the philosopher Peter Singer. "If I am walking past a shallow pond and see a child drowning in it, I ought to wade in and pull the child out," Singer wrote. "This will mean getting my clothes muddy, but this is insignificant, while the death of the child would presumably be a very bad thing."[5] And Unger has developed various kindred cases to focus our intuitions. Suppose you've spent a great deal of your limited time and means in restoring a vintage Mercedes sedan to mint condition, with particular attention to the leather upholstery, and you pass by a hiker with a badly injured foot. Though the injury isn't life threatening, he'll lose his foot if you don't take him to the hospital. There's nobody else around. Wouldn't you do it, even though the bleeding from his wound would ruin the leather seat? Then suppose you received an envelope from UNICEF asking for a donation for thirty children in a foreign land; if you don't send a hundred dollars, they will die. Tossing the envelope in the trash is, in a similar way, immoral.

But, of course, if that's true for the first hundred dollars you could give, it's true for the next hundred dollars you could give. That's why Unger can conclude that "it's seriously wrong not to send to the likes of UNICEF and OXFAM, about as promptly as possible, nearly all your worldly wealth."[6] You'd have to liquidate your assets and empty your coffers until you could be sure that your losing a hundred dollars was worse than thirty kids' dying. Robert Sibley is at the back of the room, rightly shaking his head in disbelief. What has gone wrong?

Let me make, first, a small but important point. All this talk of mandarins and foreign children can make it seem that Unger's paradox is a special problem for cosmopolitans. It is not. Forget the starving children of Africa and Asia, if you can. Wherever you live in the West, there are children's lives to be saved in your own country. There are fewer of them, and saving each of them will cost more: but should your response to the drowning child depend on the cost of your suit? There are also—need I mention?—adults you wouldn't leave to die in a puddle either. You could give some of them longer lives, lives they want, by paying their medical bills. If you live in a metropolitan area, there are some close by; they are your neighbors. Should you give away most of your money to do so? Philosophers like Unger and Singer would say yes . . . or at least they would if they didn't think the needs of the starving children elsewhere were more urgent. The problem with the argument isn't that it says we have incredible obligations to foreigners; the problem is that it claims we have incredible obligations. Whatever has gone wrong, you can't blame it on us cosmopolitans.

How does Unger get us from where we are to where he wants us to be? By starting with that drowning child. No decent person will want to conclude that not muddying my trousers justifies letting a child drown, not even if my suit was hand-tailored in mohair in Savile Row. But to go anywhere with this judgment about a particular case, you have to draw a moral; and clearly how far you can get will depend on exactly which moral you draw. Unger's most extreme statements require both drawing a very general principle and making some strong empirical assumptions. I think that both the principle and the assumptions are wrong.

Here's a principle that connects the drowning child to the conclusions I quoted above.

> If you can prevent something bad from happening at the cost of something less bad, you ought to do it.

There seems, at first, no doubt that this principle—which, since it appears to motivate some of Peter Singer's arguments, I'll call the Singer principle—has the consequence that you should save the drowning child.[7] The child's drowning is bad; getting your suit dirty is much less bad. All this I grant. But does our moral response to the drowning child really entail giving away all our worldly wealth?

The Singer principle requires you to prevent bad things from happening if the cost is something less awful. Upon reflection, however, it's not so clear that the principle even gets the drowning case right. Saving the child may be preventing something bad; but *not* saving the child might, for all we know, prevent something worse. After all, shouldn't I be busy about saving those hundreds of thousands of starving children? And wouldn't selling my suit raise a few hundred dollars? And wouldn't ruining it mean I couldn't raise those dollars? The principle says that, if this kid right here has to drown for me to save my suit for sale so I can save, say, ninety other children, so be it; though it also leaves me free to let the ninety die, if I can find something worse to prevent. As for that hiker with the bleeding foot, he's plainly out of luck: why hurt the sedan's resale value, given all the good in the world we could do with the money? The seeming moderation of the principle hides a powerful claim: it's really a way of saying you should do the most you can to minimize the amount of badness in the world. I have no idea how I would do that. But there's no reason to think it involves bankrupting myself to send a large check to UNICEF. There's bound to be at least one thing I can do with the money that would do more good. The problem would be working out what that was.

The larger point, of course, is that our conviction that we should save the drowning child doesn't by itself tell us *why* we should do so. I have already argued that our moral intuitions are often more secure than the principles we appeal to in explaining them. There are countless principles that would get you to save the drowning child without justifying your own immiseration. Here's one:

> If you are the person in the best position to prevent something really awful, and it won't cost you much to do so, do it.

Now this principle—which I am inclined, for the moment, to think may be right—simply doesn't have the radical consequences of the Singer principle. I'm not especially well placed to save the children that UNICEF has told me about. And even if I were, giving away most of my means would radically reduce my quality of life. Perhaps this principle suggests that Bill Gates should give millions to save poor children from dying around the world. But, come to think of it, he does that already.

This principle—I'll call it the emergency principle—is a low-level one that I think is pretty plausible. I wouldn't be surprised, though, if some philosopher came up with a case where the emergency principle gave what I thought was the wrong answer. That's because figuring out moral principles, as an idle glance at the history of moral philosophy will show you, is *hard*. I have talked often in this book about values, in part because I think it is easier to identify values than to identify exceptionless principles. One reason that life is full of hard decisions is precisely that it's not easy to identify single principles, like the Singer principle, that aim to tell you what to do. (Even the Singer principle tells you what to do only if you can reduce all values to their contributions to the badness in the world, which is something I seriously doubt.) Another reason is that it's often unclear what the effects will be of what we do.

On the other hand, many decisions *aren't* so hard, because some of our firmest moral knowledge is about particular cases. I have no doubt at all that I should save the drowning child and ruin my suit. (Oddly, American states differ as to whether this requirement is a legal one.) There are many arguments that I might make in defense of this view, especially to someone who was seriously convinced that he was free to let the child drown. But I am less certain of most of those arguments than I am that I should save the child.

Basic Needs

The emergency principle may or may not be sound, but it tells me nothing about what I should do when UNICEF sends me a request for money. I think that a cosmopolitan who believes that every human being matters cannot be satisfied with that. So let's start with the sort of core moral ideas increasingly articulated in our conception of basic human rights.[8] People have needs—health, food, shelter, education—that must be met if they are to lead decent lives. There are certain options that they ought to have: to seek sexual satisfaction with consenting partners; to have children if they wish to; to move from place to place; to express and share ideas; to help manage their societies; to exercise their imaginations. (These are options. People should also be free not to exercise them.) And there are certain obstacles to a good life that ought not to be imposed upon them: needless pain, unwarranted contempt, the mutilation of their bodies. To recognize that everybody is entitled, where possible, to have their basic needs met, to exercise certain human capabilities, and to be protected from certain harms, is not yet to say how all these things are to be assured. But if you accept that these basic needs ought to be met, what obligations have you incurred? I want to offer some constraints on an acceptable answer.

First, the primary mechanism for ensuring these entitlements remains the nation-state. There are a few political cosmopolitans who say they want a world government. But the cosmopolitanism I am defending prizes a variety of political arrangements, provided, of course, each state grants every individual what he or she deserves. A global state would have at least three obvious problems. It could easily accumulate uncontrollable power, which it might use to do great harm; it would often be unresponsive to local needs; and it would almost certainly reduce the variety of institutional experimentation from which all of us can learn. Accepting the nation-state means accepting that we have a special responsibility for the life and the justice of our own; but we still have to play our part in ensuring that all states respect the rights and meet the needs of their citizens. If they cannot, then all of us—through our nations, if they will do it, and in spite of them, if they won't—share the collective obligation to change them; and if the reason they fail their citizens is that they lack resources, providing resources can be part of that collective obligation. That is an equally fundamental cosmopolitan commitment.

But, second, our obligation is not to carry the whole burden alone. Each of us should do our fair share; but we cannot be required to do more. This is a constraint, however inchoate, that the Shallow Pond theorists do not respect. The Singer principle just doesn't begin to capture the subtlety of our actual moral thought. A different philosopher's story, this one offered by Richard W. Miller, makes the point. An adult is plummeting from a tenth-story window, and you, on the sidewalk below, know that you can save that person's life by cushioning his fall. If you did so, however, you would very likely suffer broken bones, which would heal, perhaps painfully and imperfectly, over a period of months. (Suppose you know all this because you're an orthopedic surgeon.) To Miller it's clear that you can do your "fair share in making the world a better place while turning down this chance for world-improvement."[9] Since the death you failed to prevent is worse than a few months of suffering, the Singer principle, of course, says otherwise. Our ordinary moral thinking makes distinctions the principle doesn't capture.

Now, I agree that it's not easy to specify what our fair share might be, and especially how it might be affected by the derelictions of others. Suppose we had a plan for guaranteeing everyone his or her basic entitlements. Let's call the share that I owe— suppose it would be paid as a development tax—my basic obligation. Even if we could get everyone to agree on the virtues of the plan; and even if we could determine how each of us, depending on our resources, should contribute his or her fair share, we can be pretty confident that some people would not give their fair share. That means there would still be some unmet entitlements. What is the obligation of those who have already met their basic obligation? Is it enough simply to say, "I know there are unmet entitlements, but I have done my part"? After all, the unmet entitlements are still unmet, and they're still entitlements.

Third, whatever our basic obligations, they must be consistent with our being, as I said at the beginning, partial to those closest to us: to our families, our friends, our nations; to the many groups that call upon us through our identities, chosen and unchosen; and, of course, to ourselves. Whatever my basic obligations are to the poor far away, they cannot be enough, I believe, to trump my concerns for my family, my friends, my country; nor can an argument that every life matters require me to be indifferent to the fact that one of those lives is mine. This constraint is another that the Shallow Pond theorists are indifferent toward. They think that it is so important to avoid the bad things in other lives that we should be willing to accept for ourselves, our families and friends, lives that are barely worth living. This third constraint interacts, I think, with the worry that I expressed about the second. For if so many people in the world are not doing their share—and they clearly are not—it seems to me I cannot be required to derail my life to take up the slack.

Let me add one final, general constraint. Any plausible answer to the question of what we owe to others will have to take account of many values; no sensible story of our obligations to strangers can ignore the diversity of the things that matter in human life. Cosmopolitans, more than anyone else, know this. Imagine a drab totalitarian regime with excellent prenatal healthcare. After a "velvet revolution," a vibrant democracy emerges and freedom reigns. But perhaps because the health care system is a little wobblier (or perhaps because some pregnant mothers exercise their newly won right to smoke and drink), the rates of infant mortality are a little higher. Most people would still plump for the velvet revolution. We think the death of a child is a very bad thing; but clearly we don't think it's the only thing that matters. This is part of why the child in the pond isn't adequate to the real complexity of our thinking.

What would the world look like if people always spent their money to alleviate diarrhea in the Third World and never on a ticket to the opera (or a donation to a local theater company, gallery, symphony orchestra, library, or what have you)? Well, it would probably be a flat and dreary place. You do not need to say—as Unger would invite you to—that the lives of the children you could have saved were just worth less than your evening at the ballet. That answer presupposes that there is really only one thing that matters: that all values are measurable in a single thin currency of goodness and badness. It was terribly wrong that slaves were worked to death building the pyramids—or, for that matter, in building the United States—but it is not therefore terrible that those monuments, or this nation, exist. Not all values have a single measure. If the founders of this nation had dealt only with the most urgent moral problem facing them—and let us suppose that it was, indeed, slavery—they would almost certainly not have set in motion the slow march of political, cultural, and moral progress, with its sallies and its retreats, that Americans justly take pride in. Would you really want to live in a world in which the only thing anyone had ever cared about was saving lives?

Decisions, Decisions

I realize that, to some, what I have just said is shocking. I have defended going to the opera when children are dying, children who could be saved with the price of admission. It is, perhaps, almost as counterintuitive to say this as it is to say, with Unger, that we should sacrifice nearly everything else we value to save the poor. So remember, when you go to the opera, others are spending money, too; money that could save the same children. You have no special relationship to their deaths, as you would if you ignored the emergency principle. Nor is this like willing the mandarin to death. You are not killing anyone by going to the opera. Part of the strategy of Unger's argument is to persuade us that not intervening to save someone because we have something else worth doing is morally equivalent to killing him in the name of those other values. We should resist the equation.

But the Shallow Pond arguments raise more empirical concerns, to which, as I promised, I now return. Consider the factual claim that UNICEF can save the lives of thirty children for $100. What does this mean? It doesn't, of course, mean that you can keep them alive forever. Part of the reason UNICEF or OXFAM—both well-run organizations full of well-intentioned people doing much good—can keep sending those letters is that they have to save the same children over and over again. You send the check. Even if, *per impossibile*, your money could be traced to a particular village in Bangladesh, rehydrating thirty particular children who would otherwise have died of their diarrhea, you are not thereby making a serious contribution to the real improvement of their life chances. Death isn't the only thing that matters. What matters is decent lives. And if what you save them for is just another month or another year or another decade of horrible suffering, have you really made the best use of your money? Indeed, have you really made the world less bad?

This isn't to criticize the particular organizations that Unger has chosen to celebrate. I am confident that they, and organizations like them, are doing much genuine long-term good. But responding to the crisis of a child dying because her frail body cannot absorb fluids faster than they pour out of her is not really saving her, if tomorrow she will eat the same poor food, drink the same infected water, and live in a country with the same incompetent government; if the government's economic policies continue to block real development for her family and her community; if her country is still trapped in poverty in part because our government has imposed tariffs on some of their exports to protect American manufacturers with a well-organized lobbying group in Washington, while the European Union saves jobs for its people by placing quotas on the importation of others.

A genuinely cosmopolitan response begins with caring to try to understand *why* that child is dying. Cosmopolitanism is about intelligence and curiosity as well as engagement. It requires knowing that policies that I might have supported because they protect jobs in my state or region are part of the answer. It involves seeing not just a suffering body but a wasted human life.

Once you start thinking about the facts—which play a large role in Singer's arguments, but rather little in Unger's—the dilemmas about intervention proliferate. There are, to begin with, problems of timing. If Bill Gates had followed Peter Unger's advice when he was in his twenties, he wouldn't have been in a position to give billions to good causes today. He didn't know that he'd be a billionaire, of course. (He thought he would be, no doubt, that's the way with entrepreneurs; but he didn't *know*.) One of the things wealth is good for is generating more wealth. I can probably do more good later by saving and investing now. Peter Singer would tell me that, if that's my argument, I should be saving and investing more. But that would mean less expenditure now; fewer people— some of them in the poorest countries of the world—would be earning dollars by making the goods and providing the services I pay for. Indeed, if all Americans or Europeans stopped buying consumer goods, the result would almost certainly be a collapse of the global economy. Government income from taxation would fall, and government development assistance would fall with it. Given the role of consumption in driving the American economy, creating the wealth that the U.S. government taxes in order to pay, among other things, for development assistance, you'd have to be a pretty good economist to figure out whether Singer was right.

Once you take seriously the real challenges posed by global poverty, you have to come to grips with hard problems about how money is best spent. Given the results, most development economists would agree that much of the trillion dollars in foreign aid between 1950 and 1995 wasn't well spent. After all, many of the poorest countries in the world have seen incomes *fall* over that period.[10] That's not a reason for giving up, though. It's a reason for trying to understand what went wrong and what went right—especially in the places, like Botswana, where aid really helped—and reapplying ourselves to the task.

There are questions to do with technological advances that may yet come. Take AIDS in Africa. Should we invest heavily in the distribution of antiretrovirals to extend the lives of those currently living with HIV/AIDS? Or should the priority be vaccine research, in the hopes of preventing or mitigating future infections? We'll want to invest in health care infrastructure, clean water, education, water, clinics, and roads to get to them—but which should get priority? And if we do build the roads, which will help get the nurses and the doctors to the clinics, will they have the resources, not just the money but the people with the knowledge, to maintain them? Part of what it means for an economy to be, as we used to say, underdeveloped is that there are limits on how fast it can absorb capital.

In recent years, social scientists have increasingly recognized that a crucial constraint on development is weak governance and poor institutions. The Nobel Prize–winning economist Amartya Sen famously showed that, while famine can be triggered by nature—a drought, a plague of locusts—it doesn't occur in democracies. According to a recent study by the economists Craig Burnside and David Dollar, foreign assistance helped development and reduced poverty—but only in countries with decent policies.[11] Institutions of land tenure, which are often intertwined with cultural assumptions that may be hard to change, are sometimes at the root of rural poverty. In Asante, land is held by local chiefs "in trust" for the people. To fertilize, sow, and cultivate my land, I may need to borrow. But if I farm on the land at the chief's discretion, how can I secure a debt? Clear title may require reform of land law, establishing reliable land registers and making the courts more efficient and less corrupt. I know, gentle reader, that you will pay to send food to starving children. Will you pay to promote reform in the design and execution of the land policies that help keep their families poor?

I am not arguing—I do not believe—that we should throw up our hands in despair. Nor do I think that because past aid has not raised the standard of living in much of Africa, we should abandon attempts to help. We are not in danger of being excessively generous; indeed, most of us are in no danger of meeting what I called our basic obligation. But what's wanted, as Adam Smith would have anticipated, is the exercise of reason, not just explosions of feeling. Charitable giving in the wake of the tsunami of Christmas 2004 was remarkable and heartening; but two million people die each year of malaria; 240,000 a month die of AIDS; 136,000 of diarrhea.[12] And practical-minded economists, like Jeffrey Sachs, starting with real data, have made arguments that really concerted and well-orchestrated efforts to alleviate poverty in the Third World have a good shot at success. They rebut the usual defeatist assumptions. Too many people, for example, are reflex Malthusians, worried that saving hungry children can only result in more hungry adults. But that depends on how you do it. If you save children by creating opportunities for their parents and so raising overall affluence, then, history affirms, fertility rates ultimately decline. On the other hand, if you "save" the children by dumping free grain into the local economy and putting the local farmers out of business—who can compete with free?— you may, indeed, be doing more harm than good.

U.S. government foreign aid was a little over $16 billion in 2003; American private assistance to low-income countries was at least $6.3 billion in the same year.[13] The American development assistance budget is the largest in the world. As a percentage of GDP, though, it is at the bottom of the affluent donor nations. Many poor countries pay more in debt servicing to the United States than they receive in assistance; and, in turn, much of that assistance merely takes the form of debt relief. Only a fraction of American foreign assistance is specifically targeted at helping the extremely poor. These numbers, however, obscure other things, both for better and for worse, that America does. For example, on the debit side, U.S. tariffs cost the tsunami-affected countries more in 2004—about $1.8 billion—than U.S. charity will enrich them, though American trade policies are generally much better for the developing world than those of Europe or Japan.[14] (James Wolfensohn, the former president of the World Bank, once pointed out that "the average European cow lives on $2.50-a-day subsidy when three billion people live on under $2 a day.") On the credit side, America admits many more immigrants than Japan and Europe, and those immigrants send tens of billions home in remittances, creating, at least potentially, a savings base for capital and growth. On the debit side again, however, the United States is meeting its health needs—especially those of poor Americans—with a brain drain of doctors and nurses (trained, usually, at public expense), from places like India, Pakistan, Ghana, Nigeria, and Jamaica, where they are desperately needed.

When you spend your dollars—or euros or pounds—isn't it worth also spending a moment or two to ask whether they are being spent intelligently? However much you give, doesn't it matter that none of it is wasted? Part of the trouble with Peter Unger's focus on those starving children is that it blocks thought about the complexity of the problems facing the global poor. Ask the people at

OXFAM and UNICEF whether they think that all that matters is keeping children alive a while longer.

The juxtaposition of Western affluence with Third World poverty can sometimes lead activists to see the two as causally linked in some straightforward way, as if they are poor because we are rich. So it's worth remembering that poverty is far less prevalent today than it was a century ago. Since 1950, life expectancy and literacy rates in the developing world have increased quite dramatically. In 1990, some 375 million people in China were living in what the World Bank calls "extreme poverty," an income of less than a dollar a day. By 2001, that figure declined by more than 160 million, even as the total population continued to rise. The number of South Asians living in extreme poverty declined by tens of millions. But Africa has been left behind, and it is Africa that presents the greatest challenge to our development experts—and to our sense of our global obligations.

In thinking about trade policies, immigration policies, and aid policies, in deciding which industries to subsidize at home, which governments to support and arm abroad, politicians in the world's richest countries naturally respond most to the needs of those who elected them. But they should be responding to their citizens' aspirations as well. And America's attitude toward foreign assistance is a complicated thing. In surveys, American are apt to say that too much is given; and then propose that the amount be lowered, say, to just 5 percent of the federal budget. (That's ten times more than the United States actually allocated in 2005.) Some decades ago, the great development economist Alfred O. Hirschman, in a paper he wrote with Richard M. Bird, made an arresting proposal. Suppose you allowed taxpayers to specify that a certain amount of what they paid (up to 5 percent, the economists suggested) be designated for foreign aid contributions, remitted to a World Development Fund. The proposal had various embellishments, but one result, they recognized, would be this: "we would have, for the first time, a concrete indication of how many people in the United States care enough about foreign aid to be willing explicitly to divert some of their tax dollars to it. Our initial assumption is that more aid is a good thing. This proposal would, if nothing else, enable us to know how many people agree with us."[15]

As I say, I do not know exactly what the basic obligations are of each American or each human being. A few years ago, the UN convened a summit meeting in Monterrey, Mexico, in which leaders from all over discussed specific ways of alleviating the kind of grinding poverty that afflicts a sixth of the world's population. Needless to say, the announced goals, itemized in the "Monterrey consensus," haven't been met—agreeing on where you want to go doesn't get you there—but it was a truly cosmopolitan conversation on a matter of central cosmopolitan concern. It's important that conversations like these continue; it's even more important that they don't remain just at the level of conversation. For if there are people without their basic entitlements—and there are billions of them—we know that, collectively, we are not meeting our obligations. The Shallow Pond theorists are wrong about what we owe. They are surely right to insist that we owe more.

Faced with impossible demands, we are likely to throw up our hands in horror. But the obligations we have are not monstrous or unreasonable. They do not require us to abandon our own lives. They entail, as Adam Smith saw, clearheadedness, not heroism. Jeffrey Sachs has argued that in twenty years, at a cost of about $150 billion a year, we can eradicate extreme poverty—the poverty that kills people and empties lives of meaning. I don't know whether the number is correct or whether his detailed proposals are, either. But if he is even half right, the richest nations can together salvage the wasted lives of the poorest human beings, by spending collectively less than a third of what the United States spends each year on defense all by itself; put another way, we could raise the money at about 45 cents a day for each citizen of the European Union, the United States, Canada, and Japan which is a little more than a third of what the average Norwegian is paying already. The average Norwegian is not three times richer than the average citizen of the industrialized world.[16] If we accept the cosmopolitan challenge, we will tell our representatives that we want them to remember those strangers. Not because we are moved by their suffering—we may or may not be—but because we are responsive to what Adam Smith called "reason, principle, conscience, the inhabitant of the breast." The people of the richest nations can do better. This is a demand of simple morality. But it is one that will resonate more widely if we make our civilization more cosmopolitan.

And, not to leave you in any suspense about it, Rastignac's friend, too, was guided by that inhabitant of the breast. "Damn it," he said, after some brow-furrowing thought. "I've come to the conclusion that the Chinaman must live."

ACKNOWLEDGMENTS

Thanks to Skip Gates for inviting me to write this book and for his friendship over many years. Also to Josh Cohen and Martha Nussbaum, who started me out thinking about philosophical cosmopolitanism some years ago. Conversations with Mark Johnston, Steve Macedo, Gil Harman, Peter Singer, and Jon Haidt influenced my thinking at various crucial stages (though none of them, alas, can be held responsible for what I did with their ideas). I am very grateful to all at Norton, especially Bob Weil, for being a patient, swift, and helpful editor, Roby Harrington, especially for help with the original concept, and Eleen Chung, for designing the jacket. Thanks to Karen Dalton for leading us to the Tiepolo on the cover. I'd also like to thank my sisters and my brothers-in-law for introducing me to Namibia, Nigeria, and Norway and a whole lot else; and my cousins around the world for teaching me, over the decades, about the places they know.

As always, in this as in all things, my greatest debt is to my partner Henry Finder, *sine quo non*.

My thanks to my mother are already expressed on the dedication page; but I can't resist telling one short story about why this seems to me so much her book. My mother moved to Ghana in 1955. When my father died in 1990, people kept asking her when she was going home. "But I *am* home," she always said. Then she had an idea. She went to the City Council offices and bought the plot next to the one where my father was buried and had it covered with a concrete slab; just to make sure no one else was buried there first. Now, when anyone asks, she says, "I've got my burial plot here in Kumasi." As I write these words, fifty years after my mother moved from England, she's still at home in Kumasi.

NOTES

Introduction

1. Galatians 3:28. In quoting the Bible, I have used the King James version, except for the Pentateuch, where I have used Robert Alter's powerful modern translation, *The Five Books of Moses* (New York: Norton, 2004).

2. Cristoph Martin Wieland, "Das Geheimniß des Kosmopolitenordens," *Teutscher Merkur*, August 1788, p. 107. (Where I give a reference only to a source that is not in English, the translation is mine.)

3. *Essai sur les mœurs et l'esprit des nations,* vol. 16 of *Oeuvres complètes de Voltaire* (Paris: L'Imprimerie de la Société Litteraire-Typographique, 1784), p. 241. Voltaire is speaking specifically here of "the Orient," and especially of China and India, but he would surely not have denied its more general application.

4. George Eliot, *Daniel Deronda* (London: Penguin, 1995), pp. 745, 661–62, 183.

5. Cicero, *De officiis* 1.50.

Chapter 1. The Shattered Mirror

1. *The Romance of Isabel Lady Burton*, ed. by W. H. Wilkins, vol. 2 (New York: Dodd Mead, 1897), p. 712.

2. Homer, *The Odyssey,* trans. Robert Fitzgerald (New York: Farrar, Straus and Giroux, 1998), p. 55.

3. Herodotus, *The Histories,* trans. Aubrey de Sélincourt, rev. John Marincola (London: Penguin, 1996), pp. 12, 14.

4. Richard F. Burton, *To the Gold Coast for Gold* (London: Chatto and Windus, 1883), p. 59.

5. *Blackwood's Edinburgh Magazine* 83 (February 1858): 222; (March 1858): 276, 289; (February 1858): 220.

6. Richard F. Burton, *The City of the Saints and across the Rocky Mountains to California* (New York: Harper and Brothers, 1862), pp. 38, 152, 36, 446, 404–10.

Chapter 2. The Escape from Positivism

1. Herodotus, *The Histories,* trans. Aubrey de Sélincourt, rev. John Marincola (London: Penguin, 1996), p. 169.

2. "Hadji Murat," in Leo Tolstoy, *Master and Man and Other Stories*, trans. Paul Foote (London: Penguin, 1977), p. 240.

3. William G. Sumner, *Folkways* (Boston: Atheneum Press, 1907), p. 331.

4. Melville J. Herskovits, *Cultural Relativism* (New York: Random House, 1973), p. 56.

Chapter 4. Moral Disagreements

1. Michael Walzer, *Thick and Thin: Moral Arguments at Home and Abroad* (Notre Dame: University of Notre Dame Press, 1994).

2. See Paul Rozin, "Food Is Fundamental, Fun, Frightening, and Far-reaching," *Social Research* 66 (1999): 9–30. I am grateful to John Haidt for a discussion of these issues.

3. Leviticus 18:22 and 20:13.

4. Menstruation: Leviticus 15:19–28. Male ejaculation: Leviticus 15:16–18.

5. Leviticus 17:11–13. In a footnote (p. 618), Alter suggests what the content of this explanation really amounts to. The proscription itself is in the preceding verse.

6. H. L. A. Hart introduced the idea of "open texture" to discussions of jurisprudence in *The Concept of Law* (Oxford: Clarendon Press, 1997), chap. 6. He borrowed the idea of open texture from F. Waismann, who thought open texture was an irreducible feature of language. The example of the bylaw about vehicles in the park is Hart's; see his "Positivism and the Separation of Law and Morals," *Harvard Law Review* 71 (1958): 593–629.

7. W. B. Gallie, "Essentially Contested Concepts," *Proceedings of the Aristotelian Society* 56 (1956): 169.

8. Charles L. Black Jr., *Capital Punishment: The Inevitability of Caprice and Mistake,* 2d ed. (New York: Norton, 1981).

Chapter 5. The Primacy of Practice

1. Cass R. Sunstein, "Incompletely Theorized Agreements," *Harvard Law Review* 108 (1995): 1733–72.

2. Joseph Appiah, *Joe Appiah: The Autobiography of an African Patriot* (New York: Praeger, 1990), p. 22.

3. I have put this complaint in the mouth of a Muslim. But the truth is you could hear it from non-Muslims in many places as well. It is less likely to be heard in non-Muslim Africa, because there, by and large (as Amartya Sen has pointed out), women have a less unequal place in public life. See Jean Drèze and Amartya Sen, *Hunger and Public Action* (Oxford: Clarendon Press, 1989).

Chapter 6. Imaginary Strangers

1. Brent Berlin and Paul Kay, *Basic Color Terms: Their Universality and Evolution* (Berkeley: University of California Press, 1969).

2. Donald Brown, *Human Universals* (Boston: McGraw-Hill, 1991).

Chapter 7. Cosmopolitan Contamination

1. John Stuart Mill, *On Liberty*, in *Essays on Politics and Society*, ed. John M. Robson, vol. 18 of *The Collected Works of John Stuart Mill* (Toronto: University of Toronto Press, 1977), p. 270.

2. Quoted in Larry Strelitz, "Where the Global Meets the Local: Media Studies and the Myth of Cultural Homogenization," *Transnational Broadcasting Studies*, no. 6 (Spring/Summer 2001), http://www.tbsjournal.com/Archives/Spring01/strelitz.html.

3. Ien Ang, *Watching "Dallas": Soap Opera and the Melodramatic Imagination* (London: Methuen, 1985); Tamar Liebes and Elihu Katz, *The Export of Meaning: Cross-cultural Readings of Dallas* (New York: Oxford University Press, 1990); John Sinclair, Elizabeth Jacka, and Stuart Cunningham, eds., *New Patterns in Global Television: Peripheral Vision* (New York: Oxford University Press, 1996); Rob Nixon, *Homelands, Harlem and Hollywood: South African Culture and the World Beyond* (New York: Routledge, 1994); Strelitz, "Where the Global Meets the Local."

4. See J. D. Straubhaar, "Beyond Media Imperialism: Asymmetrical Interdependence and Cultural Proximity," *Critical Studies in Mass Communications* 8 (1991): 39–59.

5. The quotes from the Zulu student Sipho are from Larry Strelitz *Where the Global Meets the Local: South African Youth and Their Experience of the Global Media* (PhD Thesis, Rhodes University, 2003), pp. 137–41.

6. Salman Rushdie, *Imaginary Homelands: Essays and Criticism, 1981–1991* (London: Granta Books, 1991), p. 394.

Chapter 8. Whose Culture Is It, Anyway?

1. Ivor Wilks, *Asante in the Nineteenth Century: The Structure and Evolution of a Political Order* (Cambridge: Cambridge University Press, 1975). The history of Asante in the nineteenth century has a great deal to do with its wars and treaties with Britain. Sir Garnet Wolseley's sack of Kumasi was intended to establish British dominance in the region; though the fact is that he entered Kumasi unopposed on February 4, 1874, and had to retreat two days later because he needed to take his sick and wounded back to the safety of the Gold Coast colony. The expedition of 1895–96, in which Baden-Powell took part, was intended in part to enforce the settlement of 1874 and to establish British sovereignty over Asante by the forced submission of the king. The British eventually exiled a number of political leaders, like the Asantehene, to the Seychelles, remote islands in the middle of the Indian

Ocean, in order to make it hard for them to communicate with their peoples. Prempeh I returned to the Gold Coast colony as a private citizen in 1924, and was allowed to resume his title as Kumasehene—the chief of Kumasi—a couple of years later. Only in 1935 was his successor, Osei Agyeman Prempeh II (my great-uncle by marriage), allowed to resume the title of Asantehene, king of Asante.

2. I owe a great deal to the cogent (and cosmopolitan!) outline of the development of the relevant international law in John Henry Merryman's classic paper "Two Ways of Thinking about Cultural Property," *American Journal of International Law* 80, no. 4 (October 1986): 831–53.

3. James Cuno, "U.S. Art Museums and Cultural Property," *Connecticut Journal of International Law 16* (Spring 2001): 189–96.

4. Michael F. Brown, "Can Culture Be Copyrighted?" *Current Anthropology* 39, no. 2 (April 1998): 203.

5. Lawrence Lessig, *Free Culture: How Big Media Uses Technology and the Law to Lock Down Culture and Control Creativity* (New York: Penguin Press, 2004).

6. Merryman, "Two Ways of Thinking," p. 852.

7. The quotations from the *Daily Telegraph*, London *Times*, and *New York Herald*, as well as the information about Osei Bonsu, are all from Wilks, *Asante in the Nineteenth Century*, pp. 200–201.

Chapter 9. The Counter-Cosmopolitans

1. Olivier Roy, *Globalized Islam: The Search for a New Ummah* (New York: Columbia University Press, 2004), p. 25. Though published in the United States, the book uses (mostly) British spelling. I have silently Americanized it for the convenience of the reader.

2. *Ibid.* p. 149.

3. Jeffrey Gettleman with David M. Halbfinger, "Suspect in '96 Olympic Bombing and 3 Other Attacks Is Caught," *New York Times*, June 1, 2003, p. 1.

4. For Sayyid Ahmad Khan see the essay by Javed Majeed in *Islam and Modernity: Muslim Intellectuals Respond* (London: I. B. Tauris, 2000); for Taha see the essay by Mohamed Mahmoud; there are references to Muhammad 'Abduh throughout the book. And see Tariq Ramadan, *Western Muslims and the Future of Islam* (New York: Oxford University Press, 2003); Khaled Abou El-Fadl, *The Place of Tolerance in Islam* (Boston: Beacon Press, 2002).

5. See the interview by Rania Al Malky in *Egypt Today*, 26, no. 2 (February 2005).

6. *The Koran*, trans. N. J. Dawood (London: Penguin , 2002) 29:46; 2:256.

7. Bernard Williams, *Ethics and the Limits of Philosophy* (Cambridge: Harvard University Press, 1985), p. 174.

8. Burke, *Reflections on the Revolution in France*, ed. J. C. D. Clark (Stanford: Stanford University Press, 2001), p. 202.

Chapter 10. Kindness to Strangers

1. Honoré de Balzac, *Père Goriot* (Paris: Éditions Garniers Frères, 1961), pp. 154–55. (A footnote in this edition suggests that Balzac got the mandarin from Chateaubriand, who certainly knew his Smith.)

2. Adam Smith, *The Theory of Moral Sentiments,* ed. Knud Haakonssen (Cambridge: Cambridge University Press, 2002), p. 157. The chapter is entitled "Of the Influence and Authority of Conscience."

3. Robert Sibley, "Globalization and the Meaning of Canadian Life," *Canadian Review of Books*, 28, nos. 8–9 (Winter 2000).

4. Peter Unger, *Living High and Letting Die: Our Illusion of Innocence* (New York: Oxford University Press, 1996), p. 56.

5. Peter Singer, "Famine, Affluence, and Morality," *Philosophy and Public Affairs*, 1, no. 3 (Spring 1972): 231.

6. Unger, *Living High,* p. 143.

7. Singer's own formulation is this: "if it is in our power to prevent something bad from happening, without thereby sacrificing anything of comparable moral importance, we ought, morally, to do it. By 'without sacrificing anything of comparable moral importance,' I mean without causing anything else comparably bad to happen, or doing something that is wrong in itself, or failing to promote some moral good, comparable in significance to the bad thing that we can prevent." Singer, "Famine," p. 231.

8. I am attracted to the way of defining what we are entitled to that is to be found in Martha C. Nussbaum, "Human Capabilities" in Martha C. Nussbaum and Jonathan Glover, eds. *Women, Culture, and Development: A Study of Human Capabilities* (Oxford: Clarendon Press, 1995), p. 72. For further work in this tradition see Martha C. Nussbaum and Amartya Sen, eds., *The Quality of Life* (Oxford: Oxford University Press, 1993).

9.. Richard W. Miller, "Cosmopolitan Respect and Patriotic Concern," *Philosophy and Public Affairs* 27 (1998): 209.

10. George Easterly, *The Elusive Quest for Growth: Economists' Adventures and Misadventures in the Tropics* (Cambridge: MIT Press, 2001).

11. Craig Burnside and David Dollar, "Aid, Policies, and Growth" (World Bank Policy Research Working Paper No. 569252, June 1997), http://ssrn.com/abstract= 569252.

12. David R. Francis, "U.S. Foreign Aid: Do Americans Give Enough?" *Christian Science Monitor,* January 6, 2005.

13. Steven Radelet, "Think Again: Foreign Aid," Posted on the *Foreign Policy* magazine Web site February 2005, http://www.foreignpolicy.com/story/files/story2773.php.

14. Radelet, *ibid.,* points out that promised U.S. assistance of $350 million is dwarfed by the $1.8 billion in tariffs it raises on imports from Indonesia, Sri Lanka, Thailand, and India alone.

15. Albert O. Hirschman, with Richard M. Bird, *Foreign Aid: A Critique and a Proposal*, Princeton Essays in International Finance, no. 69 (July 1968), reprinted in Hirschman, *A Bias for Hope: Essays on Development and Latin America* (New Haven: Yale University Press, 1971), p. 224.

16. Francis, "U.S. Foreign Aid."

INDEX

Aboriginal intellectual property, 128–29
abortion, 45, 80, 81–82, 142
Abou El-Fadl, Khaled, 147
abusua (matriclan), 34, 47–49, 103–4
'Adbuh, Muhammad, 146–47
adultery, 9, 10–11, 56
Africa:
    art of, 115–18, 120, 124, 125–26,
        131, 132–34
    colonization of, 2, 7, 8, 79, 80, 107,
        115–16, 132–34, 179*n*–80*n*
    debt crisis of, 171
    foreign aid to, 158–62, 168–74
    HIV/AIDS pandemic in, 42, 89, 169,
        170
    slavery in, 8
African Americans, 62, 142–43, 152, 166
Agamemnon, 65
Ahl al-Kitab (People of the Book), 150
Ahmad Khan, Sayyid, 146–47
AIDS, 38, 42, 89, 169, 170
Akan society, 26, 47–53, 69, 73, 133
Akbar (Mughal emperor), 150
akyiwadeε (taboo), 49–53, 69, 73
Al-Azhar University, 147
Alexander the Great, xii, 112
Algeria, 139
Ali, Muhammad, 102, 113
Allah, 8–10, 52, 145, 146, 147, 148,
        149, 150
Al Qaeda, 79, 138
Ami des hommes, L' (Mirabeau), xvi
Amish, xx
Analects (Confucius), 60, 63–64
Ananse stories, 29
ancestors:
    offerings to, 93–94
    worship of, 34, 52, 92–94
anthropology, 13–17, 22, 39, 50, 95, 128

Antigone, 56
anti-Semitism, xvi
Arabic language, 2, 3, 139
Arabs, 7, 11, 15, 67, 72–75, 82–83,
        109, 110, 148–49
archaeology, 117, 122, 123
Aristotle, 58–59
art, 115–35
    African, 115–18, 120, 124, 125–26,
        128–35, 131
    as cultural patrimony, 105–7,
        115–35
    destruction of, 119–22
    export licenses for, 125–26
    facsimiles of, 134–35
    international conventions on, 118,
        120–22, 125–35
    looting of, 115–16, 122–24
    market for, 115–16, 117, 118,
        122–24, 131
    nationalism and, 118–28, 131–34
    private ownership of, 122, 124–30,
        131
    provenance of, 122–24
    repatriation of, 115–16, 119, 128–35
    trusteeship of, 118–28
Asante society, 34–39, 42, 49–53, 58,
        69, 73–75, 87–90, 92, 94,
        101–5, 109, 111, 113, 115–18,
        132–34, 148–49, 170,
        179*n*–80*n*
Asante-Twi language, 90, 109
Asia, 80, 82, 98, 158–62, 172
atheism, 33–34, 141
Athens, xii, 119
authenticity, 105–7

Baden-Powell, Robert Stephenson
    Smyth, 115–16, 134, 179*n*

——— 183 ———